The Colours
of My Memories

Christie Cromwell Simmonds

Community Books

Lockeport, NS

Design: Brenda Conroy
Cover photo: Theta, Lottie & Christie
Printed and bound in Canada by
Hignell Printing, Winnipeg, MB

Copies of this book may be obtained from:
The Black Loyalist Heritage Society
PO Box 1194, 104 Birchtown Road,
Shelburne, NS, B0T 1W0
(902) 875-1310
blackloyalist@auracom.com

Published by Community Books
RR1, Lockeport, Nova Scotia, B0T 1L0
phone/fax: (902) 656-2223
email: kathleen.tudor@ns.sympatico.ca
www.selfpublishingspecialists.com

Library and Archives Canada Cataloguing in Publication

Simmonds, Christie Cromwell, 1929-2005.
The colours of my memories / Christie Cromwell Simmonds.

ISBN 1-896496-57-1

1. Simmonds, Christie Cromwell, 1929-2005. 2. Weymouth Falls (N.S.)—Biography.   3. Black Canadians—Nova Scotia—Biography.
I. Title.

FC2349.W459Z49 2006   971.6'32   C2006-903101-0

Dedicated to my grandson CJ —

Cyril James John Cromwell Simmonds —

without whose encouragement

I would never have written my story

Christie Lorraine Cromwell Simmonds

Contents

Acknowledgements

Writing this book was a very special project for Christie. She wanted to give her grandchildren, nieces and nephews some account of her memories in hopes that through this they would find glimpses of her family's life. However, Christie, as the youngest child in a family of ten, notes that these are solely her memories.

Since Christie passed away in May of 2005, many people have assisted me in the process of having her book published, and I wish to acknowledge each one. Without their help I would not have been successful in this endeavour. My heartfelt thanks go to:

Penny Anderson-Hodge (former teacher); Debra Davis-Hill, Registrar/Historian for the Black Loyalist Heritage Society; Christie's daughter Theresa Simmonds; her granddaughter Nicolle Forbes; her grandson CJ; her sisters Lottie Cromwell-States and Theta Cromwell-Jackson; her brother Everett S. Cromwell and his wife Elizabeth; Christie's nephew Winston Jackson and his wife Wanda; and Christie's cousin Marie Thomas.

— Neville Simmonds

Foreword

Reading Christie's memoirs brought back my memory of an overcrowded one-room school in Weymouth Falls, Nova Scotia, and a quiet little girl who always did her homework. Christie was a joy to teach because she always paid attention and had a desire to learn — a delight to any teacher. I did not realize then her  gift of storytelling and her ability to express herself with compassion, humour and honesty.

This book is the story of her experiences with pain: orphanhood, poverty, racism, abuse and widowhood at an early age. It also tells of her experience with joy: having loving brothers and sisters, raising her own family and being given a second opportunity of falling in love with a wonderful man, and spending her winters with him on the island of St. Kitts in the Caribbean.

The little girl born on Christmas Day grew into womanhood always believing in Santa Claus. I admired her courage and spirit, and am deeply honoured that even though I was only in her life as a teacher for a short time, whenever we met, she always called me "teacher."

— Penelope (Anderson) Hodge

Pictures from the Weymouth Falls segregated school

Irma Jarvis and her girls' morning class

Alfreda Smith and her boys' afternoon class

The Early Years

I am seventy-one years old, though I sometimes feel as young as thirty. Just when does one start to feel old anyway? One thing I have noticed, I am beginning to forget things... simple things like where I put my glasses when I have just that minute taken them off... or going from one room to another completely forgetting what I am looking for.

Cyril James John Cromwell Simmonds, my grandson, always asks me, "Why do you always love Christmas Gramma? Why do you still believe there is a Santa Claus?"

"Someday," I told him, "I will write and tell you all the reasons why. Perhaps I believe in Santa Claus — and Christmas means so much to me — because of hunger, lice and many, many other things. I will try and tell you all about it so you can understand."

Oh, how well I can remember things from way back, years ago. Perhaps this is God's plan for us, when we are old and there is nothing to keep us busy. It is time now to sit and reminisce.

I can remember so well, like it was yesterday... Mamma getting me dressed and all the many layers of clothing that we had to wear back then... bloomers, undershirt, waist (to hold up the garters for the stockings) and petticoat. All these underthings were made from cotton flour bags

9

which Mamma would have washed and bleached in the sun. It would take many washes before the bold red and blue printing of Red Rose Flour or Purity Flour would completely disappear. Then there was the cotton or flannel dress; over this we wore a pinafore, which almost completely covered the dress. Mamma called this pinafore, a "tier." All of these things were handmade by Mamma, including the moccasins, which were the shoes I wore, made of felt taken from old felt hats.

Mamma also used the secondhand clothing that would, from time to time, be sent to us from our grandmother in Boston. Many relatives from Nova Scotia had gone to the United States in search of employment, and when they found work there, they were able to send to the folks back home gifts of clothing, sometimes new, but mostly secondhand. These were very welcome in these hard times, which was right after the Great Depression. Sometimes, Mamma could afford to order new material from the Simpsons' or Eaton's catalogues.

I remember Mamma preparing for Christmas. This time of the year was the most important of all, and the house was cleaned from top to bottom very early in December. Mamma started preparing things like mincemeat, cranberry sauce, cakes and many things for the holidays. I can only recall as far back as age five or six. I was running behind Mae and Theta, supposed to be helping with the cleaning.

We sang a special song at Christmas time, as we went from room to room:

> If there's Christmas in your heart,
> If there's Christmas in your heart,
> You will walk the way of King Jesus today
> If there is Christmas in your heart.
> You will wash the dishes for your Mother
> And scrub the floor this way
> And you will share your blessings with another
> If there's Christmas in your heart.

The smells in the warm cozy kitchen are of chicken baking in the oven and on the big black iron stove a large black pot with hot oil in it for making doughnuts and the preparation of pies to be baked. The mixture of seasonings and spices combined gave the kitchen a wonderful aroma. Seated, all cozy on the old wooden lounge near the stove, would be us younger ones. In my memory it was Theta, Frankie and me, listening to the crackling of the wood fire, watching the sparks fly up through the hearth. We would not protest when sent off to bed on this night, for we wanted to go to sleep early so that morning would soon be here. Frankie usually slept in the boys' room but on this special occasion we would all jump in the bed together and talk and laugh in great anticipation — waiting for sleep to overtake us, but sleep would not come for we were all too excited.

We could hear the hustle and bustle of the rest of the family downstairs doing the last minute preparations. Many things were yet to be done. It was our tradition that the entire trimming of the tree and the living room was completed after we were sent off to bed. The tree had stood bare in the corner of the room since the day the boys brought it home from the woods. They had cut and hauled about three or four so they could pick out the best one, and there it had stood smelling of spruce or pine, waiting for the big day.

The gifts would have to be brought out from their hiding places and some even had to be wrapped. So the sounds coming from downstairs were many. Along with all the rush of preparations came talk and lots and lots of laughter when the family all got together. Suddenly, all would become quiet, and then someone would say "Listen, did you hear that?" And another would say, "Yes, I heard that. Must be Santa Claus. Let's hurry and sleep. If he finds us up he will pass and not leave anything." And we're all talking at the same time... "We must hurry up, get the place straightened up and get to bed."

Now would come the noise of rushing to finish, then all the rest of the family would come running up the stairs (this was all put on for our benefit, knowing we would all be still lying wide awake), and we would dive under the quilts, pretending to be asleep.

On Christmas Morning, one of the older boys (in my memory it was always Everett) would go downstairs first to start the fire. We would hurriedly get dressed and yell down to Everett, "Did Santa Claus come? Can we come down now?" Everett always came back with the same answer, "No, it's too cold down here and there's nothing under that old tree. Just a pail filled with ashes with a whip sticking out of it to beat bad kids with." But this answer did not discourage us; we went right on begging, "Can we come down yet?" When Everett was satisfied it was warm enough, he would call, "Come on down." Now this would start the running and scurrying and we would all pile up together there at the foot of the stairs where we would stop in our tracks to admire the great beauty, the brilliance of the completed room all aglow, with real candles burning on the side-board and the tables. The red berries, holly and ivy that had been gathered in the woods when searching for the tree were carefully wrapped around the tree, and these added to the colours of the beautiful coloured bulbs and popcorn balls.

We stood mesmerized for a time, just taking in all the beauty, before we rushed to see what was under that tree. And oh, the many gifts that would be there for everyone... toys, rag dolls, wooden horse and cart, spinning tops, games, puzzles, tin doll dishes, toy cars and trucks, usually all hand made. Some toys were bought from the stores in town, and there were lots of badly needed clothing, hand-knitted socks, mitts, scarves and hats, and many other lovely gifts.

The tradition of hanging up stockings at Christmas was not in our family, but there would be boxes for each one of us containing candy, nuts, dates, raisins, oranges, figs, bananas, coconut and many such treats that we never received during the year.

We were not to touch anything until we first went to the wooden washstand in the kitchen where stood two water buckets and a washbasin. Here we all took turns to wash our face and hands before going to the large breakfast, which was not the usual porridge, but pies, cakes, doughnuts and delicious hot drinks.

Everything we did at Christmas took lots of time. From morning till night, the day was full of excitement, fun and laughter. Family members of all ages would be heard from time to time on the floor playing with the toys. Singing, music and dancing always came with the celebration of the birth of Jesus Christ.

These are my memories and not those of the rest of my siblings; theirs most certainly must be quite different from mine. But this is me, about me, my memories. When I try to recall what my childhood was like, I find that I have blanked out the very bad times. For try as I may, I cannot recall fully the real bad scary times (they come in bits and pieces). Only the good times come to me, and they come in colour. Am I some kind of nut? My Christmas times are always pink, red and blue.

Easter in contrast is always yellow for me. Early in the morning at Easter-time, everyone would be out in our large back yard. There is a pig squealing in the pen, hens with little yellow baby chicks running behind them, and a horse named Bob. Papa would put me up on its back but I kicked and screamed. "Let her down Frankie, she's afraid!" Mamma would say. The yard is full of people, family and visiting friends. I'm feeding the chickens. This may not be just one, but many Easter Sunday mornings floating around in my memory.

Back to Christmas: on Christmas evening the family would all gather around the stove talking and still enjoying doughnuts, pies and treats of all sorts, telling stories of the past and of funny things that had happened. These were such happy and warm times, with a warm peachy glow.

As far back as I can remember they always got around to telling the following story:

Lottie, "Well I will never forget that Christmas Mamma couldn't come to the Christmas Concert because she was too sick. I had practised my lines and knew them all so well, and now I am standing there on the stage and Mamma was not there to hear how well I did my recitation. She couldn't come, she was sick." Now Lottie would look angrily at me.

Mae: "Yes and we all had to go up to Aunt Girlie and Guy's! Yes and we had to go up to Sam Langford's and stay and couldn't see what Santa Claus brought us!"

Then all would join in, "Yeah, we couldn't see what we got for Christmas or nothing! All day we had to stay away and wait!" They are all looked angrily at me.

Theta: "You know I never found that candy Mamma slapped out of my hand," she would say, cutting her eyes at me.

"Well it would have choked her," Mae put in with a sympathetic look at me.

"Well that is just what I had in mind," Theta would say with a mean laugh, "I wanted to get rid of her right off the bat." That would start the whole family howling with laughter, and they would go on and on about that Christmas.

They had to wait all morning, not having a Christmas at all until Mamma called them all into the family room. And in the bed that had been brought down from the upstairs bedroom lay Mamma, who called them each to the bed and said "Look at what Santa Claus brought you." And in the bed beside Mamma lay a little baby girl. That was the Christmas morning I, Christie Lorraine Cromwell, was born… December 25th, 1929. To this day, they never let me live it down. When we get together, they always remind me that I spoiled their Christmas the day I was born. However, throughout my life they always tried to make sure I had wonderful Christmas birthdays.

My happiest gold-coloured days were when Mamma made me molasses candy. Whenever I was unhappy or came to her crying because Theta and Mae were teasing me, or perhaps I had stubbed my toe when running barefoot through the grass, Mamma would always soothe me, taking me up in her warm, cozy, golden-brown arms... "There, there, now Cat 'n' Dog, don't cry, never mind now. Mamma will make you some molasses candy." "Cat 'n' Dog" was a nickname Mamma had given me. It came from a little song she used to sing to me. I can't recall the song, but the nickname stayed with me and to this day, my sisters call me "Cat." I would always cry when I couldn't go with the others wherever they went. Again I'd be soothed with the promise of molasses candy. This sweet treat I have come to know as taffy.

Our village was a rough hilly dirt road that ran from the town of Weymouth up through a woody area that was called Weymouth Falls. There was a small waterfall at the top, mostly hidden now by trees and bush. These falls, I was told, were used when there was a pulp mill there that employed most of the men of Weymouth and the surrounding villages.

This hilly dirt road was great in winter for coursing downhill when it was covered with snow and all iced over. It was a must to have a sled to take to school, so we could slide down one hill and course halfway up the other. Many a race was run on the way to school. In the frosty, cold evenings, most of the young people would be out on the icy hills.

The big boys made double-runners by putting a large plank on the top of two sleds, boring a hole in each of the sleds and into the plank, and bolting them together. This made one long sled, with the capacity to carry many people at one time. This made it very heavy and caused it to go much faster on the ice. Many nights there would be races down those icy hills.

Our people were the direct descendents of the Black

Loyalists, who fought the Americans for the British because of promised freedom in Nova Scotia. Some were Black Africans who had escaped their masters during slavery. On arriving in the promised land of Nova Scotia, freed Blacks encountered a wall of racism. After many years of struggle through much disappointment and hardship, they were given land but only in the most remote wooded, rocky, rough areas, with soil not suitable for agriculture.

They had no tools or help of any kind. It has been said that the authorities hoped that the Blacks would not be able to survive. After a long struggle, small lots were allotted to Blacks all over the Province of Nova Scotia, and so here in Weymouth, the wooded area of Weymouth Falls was one of these "coloured sections," as they were called, and the Cromwells were one of the Black families.

My daughter Theresa Simmonds' research has shown that there were three Cromwell brothers who settled in Weymouth Falls — Edward, Benson and Douglas. Douglas Cromwell was my grandfather. He relocated to Hassett, were he met and married Ellen Bright, of Mi'kmaw and French descent. This union produced a large family, one of whom was Frankie Cromwell, my father. Papa, I am told, was a muscular man of average height, very quiet and a little hard of hearing. He was not one to look for trouble, but if trouble found him, he could handle it and settle it. The old folks of the town told Frankie Junior and me many stories of Papa. They said that many men were afraid to start a fight with him for they could not quite understand his ways, as he was related to and brought up by people of mostly Indian decent.

Papa was well-taught — he knew how to use a bow and arrow, handle a knife and make a whistle from a tree branch, a sling shot, lash whip and much more. He knew the Mi'kmaw language and tried to teach us. He had coal-black wavy hair… a very handsome man, with both African and Indian features. Papa had such big hands he could not get them in his pockets and his habit was to walk with them just sticking in to the top of his pockets. If he was angry, he would smile, pulling his top lip tight against his teeth and ram his hands into the top of his pockets. When he did this, anyone who was trying to instigate a fight would walk away, as it was hard to know just what he would do.

We were also told that Papa and his brother, my Uncle Charlie, were pretty good fighters and could clear a room in no time, if and when a brawl broke out. Uncle Roy just loved to tell us stories of Papa and his many encounters with men who just could not figure him out, wanting to know if he could fight, but afraid to find out.

Papa met Etta Pleasant in town one day and they became friends. Etta Pleasant was the daughter of Lottie and Freeman Pleasant. The men of Weymouth Falls tried to discourage Papa from coming to the Falls to visit Mamma, because he was not from there. They told him to stay back there in Hasset and leave their woman alone, but this warning did not stop Papa. So one evening as he was walking down the Falls road, when he came to the Post Hole bridge (a spooky place with tall overhanging trees, dark and scary), standing on the bridge were three of the men of who had given him the warning to stay away. They had placed themselves at three sides of the bridge so Papa had to pass between them. Papa walked to the centre of the bridge and stood there. All three told him to go back to where he came from. They were stomping around ranting and raving, flexing their muscles and repeating their warning, demanding that Frankie Cromwell go back up the road, "Don't you dare pass here."

Papa stuck his hands in the top of his pants pockets, grinned back his famous grin with his top lip tight against his teeth, and walked around and around in circles, passing close to each of the men. Three times he did this, and then he walked on down the road to visit Mamma.

We were also told that one time at work a team of horses were pulling some logs on a flat sledge and the sledge slipped into the ditch. Two men were trying to get the sledge back onto the road, with their boss yelling and cursing at them. Now at this time Papa happened to be passing by and thought the boss was yelling to him. He stopped and assessed the situation. Then he picked up the sledge, put it up on the road and continued to walk on, leaving the boss and men standing with their mouths open. Then the boss was heard to say, "Those are the kind of blankity-blank men we have around here."

Papa was employed at the pulp mill, where he worked a hard ten-hour day. Work did not end when he got home for there were always chores to do to keep the farm going. This was a growing farm with large gardens and many fruit trees. Our land stretched back a long way through a forest to connect with the Old Tusket Road, which it was called at the time. With the help of his six growing sons, he could have made this into a large farm one day. Papa took great pride in his land and his family, instilling in them honesty, respect and all the proper things. He insisted on respect for Sunday and did not allow loud rough games to be played: on Sunday the children had to play quietly in the back yard. This did not always go well with these boys, who would often get into trouble and would often play too rough. Then one would get hurt and start bawling too loud. All would gather around the crying one, trying to sooth and comfort him so Papa would not hear.

One game was to throw a stone straight up in the air and watch where it landed and how swiftly it came down. It was Harold's turn to throw the stone. He let one go as hard as he could. Now Everett, pointing to Harold, yelled, "Look out! It's going to hit you!" Then, boink! He got it right on the top of the head. Now he is rolling around on the ground holding his head trying not to be heard crying. It was always his habit to grab his head and yell, "Oh my God," then fall down and roll on the ground. He rolled over to the well, where Guy was sitting, playing with a hammer. Guy, who was often not in the mood to be bothered, did not like to be interrupted when doing something on his own.

The others had learned to leave him alone at these times as he had a very quick temper. Harold however looked up to Guy and said, "If that was you, you would be bawling." Guy, without a word, lifted up the hammer and hit him right on the same spot the rock had landed, which sent Harold rolling and crying again.

All six boys were mischievous but Harold was the ringleader in most of their antics. Irving and Harold were often together in the mischief. Knowing that Bernard was afraid of snakes, they brought one home. One day they put it in the yard, then called Bernard, saying, "Come on out here Bernard... we have something for you." Then they had a big laugh. They told everyone how Bernard jumped really high and screamed "Mama!" when he saw the snake.

Harold even had the nerve to try talking Irving into throwing water in Papa's face. One day as Papa was sleeping with his chair leaned back by the stove, Harold got a bucket of water, and he and Irving stood debating as to who would throw the water. "You throw it." "No I don't want to throw it, you throw it..." Finally, Harold upped and let it go, right in Papa's face. They were so scared they hid behind the well, listening as Papa was raging to Mamma and asking who had thrown the water in his face. Finally, Papa came outside and finding the two boys crying behind the well and expecting to be punished, Papa stood over them a long time just staring down at them. Then he walked away.

Harold was also very mischievous at school. For instance, when Mamma sent notes to school for the teacher, Harold would tear the paper all around very close to the writing, then handing the note to the teacher would say, "Paper is scarce." From a young age was a very good artist and the teacher always chose him to do drawings on the blackboard.

Both Papa and Mamma were very strict parents though they each played games, sang and laughed with all of us and taught us all they knew. Papa could step dance and taught us all many dance steps, and even now in our old age, we will all try to strike a step when we get together. Hard work took its toll on Papa; he developed cancer of the kidneys, and after suffering many years with great pain he passed away at the early age of forty-six, leaving Mamma with ten children. The farm animals had to go and the older children left school to look for jobs. These were very hard times; the world was just recovering from the Great Depression. Times were hard for everyone, but more so for Black people.

Mamma and the children tried to keep up the home as best they could. The oldest brothers, Bernard and Irving, found work in the forestry, cutting timber, and came home on weekends. Harold became a busboy at the Goodwin Hotel (the only hotel in town). Lottie, who had already left school at the age of thirteen to work as a maid, continued working there in the town, though shortly thereafter, the family she worked for moved to Halifax and Lottie went with them. Six of us remained at home during the week: Everett, Guy (who stayed nights with our aunt), Mae, Theta, Frankie and me.

In the summer, there were berries to be picked and sold. Mamma would take us all to the fields to pick berries, and she also went to the woods with the boys who remained at home. Everett, Guy and Frankie cut pulpwood and carried it out to be stacked by the side of the road to be sold. Monies from the sale of berries and pulpwood supplemented the small amount of help Mamma received from the town. She received a small allotment of twenty-five dollars per month from the government, which she could take out in groceries at one particular store in the town.

Mamma had great patience with us and would play games or read to us in the evenings when it grew too dark to play outside. She allowed us to play games in the large kitchen and did not seem to mind no matter how wild or loud the games got. She would sit and sew or knit, watching and laughing at our antics. I can recall being a happy spoiled little girl at that time. I cannot remember exactly what

Mamma looked like but in my memory she is a heavy-set woman, with pretty brown skin, whispering softly in my ear as she combs my hair to stop me from crying. "Listen, Cat 'n' Dog, listen to the birds singing." Then she would softly sing. I remember her working... cleaning, cooking, sewing, making braided mats, and quilts. She also had beautiful flower gardens. I remember she had gotten a sewing machine from Simpsons' store on hire-purchase and was able to sew many nice clothes. She was such a good seamstress some people asked if she had purchased the outfits she made us.

Mamma had a very good sense of humour and a great laugh. When she laughed, her body shook. When the children did something bad she scolded them good, and a good switching would also be given if needed, though sometimes she would have to turn her back and laugh. However, this did not hide the fact that she was laughing, for her whole body would shake. When I really think hard and try to picture her I can just picture large warm arms, a pair of large soft knees beside my head as this person is combing my hair, a very warm feeling of great comfort and a pretty voice humming or talking or sweetly singing hymns I often hear in church to this day — "In The Sweet By and By," "Oh Beulah Land," "What a Day of Victory There Will Be," "Ninety and Nine," "I Must Tell Jesus," "Stand Up, Stand Up For Jesus."

Life for Mamma must surely have been terrible after the passing of Papa, but I was too young to understand. One winter evening when the others — Everett, Guy, Mae, Theta and Frankie — went out to course downhill, I again cried to go and had again been soothed with molasses candy, I was seated on the lounge comfortably enjoying my treat. Like in a dream my memory seems to skip, and we are now up in Mamma's room. Mamma is kneeling by the bed saying her prayers. Even though her prayer was over she was still going on mumbling things as if still talking to God. She crawled up on the bed and was moaning and groaning. I recall thinking Mamma has a tummy ache. At this same time I could hear the others coming into the porch, the noise of sledges and the dog, Caesar, barking. Mamma called them upstairs and as soon as they realized what was happening they all went into action, getting Mamma and the bed downstairs to be near the warm stove. Then Everett and Guy ran all the way to town to get Harold, who was employed as a busboy at the hotel, and to phone Lottie, who was at the time working in Halifax. I recall how frightened I was about Everett and Guy going to town in the night, in the cold. Everything was very frightening to this little girl. The confusion of all that was happening was devastating to me and it all became a period of sadness, disorder and loneliness. The house had become very quiet; time became a gray blur — not the pretty colours of happy time. It was as though our home had not been that happy, laughing, singing, joking place and this Mamma who was so jolly, who played games, cut pulpwood and sang with us was just not there. The house was always full of people — relatives and friends who came to lend a helping hand.

One day as Frankie and I were walking home from school, slowly now for we were not in a hurry to get home, we noticed a woman hanging clothes on the line. She was a stocky woman, like Mamma, and wearing a big white apron. "That's Mamma," Frankie exclaimed excitedly as he grabbed my hand and we started to run. As we got nearer, we could see it was Aunt Inez, who had come to help with the washing, as many others had done. We slowed down and strolled slowly home.

On another day when we arrived home we could hear Mamma crying. As we came in the house, we heard her saying, "They won't let me see my babies, I want to see my babies." Someone rushed me out of my coat and shoes and into the room where Mamma lay, saying in a soothing tone, "Here is Christie now, Etta. She has just come from school," and with that, they set me up on her bed. I had tried to hold back when taken to that room, as I did not like going there. It was now a scary place, no longer the happy, pretty, welcoming family room it had been. Now it was dark and gloomy, smelling of medicine, disinfectant and lilac. Someone had put a bouquet of flowers, lilac, in the room. Even now, I can't stand the smell of lilac.

There lay Mamma, not looking like Mamma at all, her once pretty brown plump face was pale, thin and grayish. She reached up a trembling arm and tried to embrace me, and with a voice that did not quite sound like hers and trying to smile she said, "Hi Cat 'n' Dog. Were you a good girl in school today? Did the teacher beat you?"

She had always asked me this. I became more at ease as we sat and talked, and so we talked and even laughed a little before I was lifted down from the bed, and it was Frankie's turn to visit with Mamma.

Mamma was taken from us shortly after. I recall lots of crying and confusion. We younger ones did not attend the funeral but were left with Mr. and Mrs. Sydney Cromwell, our neighbours. While they attended the funeral, their older children babysat us and were very kind to us, playing lovely hymns on their phonograph and feeding us lots of good food, and when the hearse went past they drew the curtains closed and we all sat very quietly. I can vaguely remember all of the brothers and sisters coming down the road after the funeral and me running and taking Bernard's hand, as we all walked down the road.

I am told that we all sat around the house for days, not even going to our beds at first — we just sat, all ten of us. What do we all do now? It was suggested by the people of the village that we be placed in the Home for Colored Children in Dartmouth, Nova Scotia. Another suggestion was that different families of the village take one of us younger ones. Each would be brought up separately by different relatives or families, but Bernard, Irving, Lottie and all the older brothers and sisters refused all of this and said, "We will try and stay together." The people of the village did not approve of this decision and they talked of all the awful things that could happen to ten children living without parents. "Nothing good will come of this," they said. "All the girls will end up having babies." Because our family did not follow all their suggestions, the people of the village disassociated themselves from us, instructing their children to stay away from our home. However, these instructions did not go down well with some of the children, who continued to come down to visit and play ball games, horseshoes, hide and seek, and what have you. There were always children in our yard.

The grant of money that had bean allotted to Mamma continued, though there was a decrease; instead of twenty-five we received fifteen dollars per month. In all of my seventy-one years, I haven't been able to figure that one out. I should think we needed an increase of money instead of a decrease. Ten orphans needed more help not less. Our uncle, Guy Pleasant, Mamma's brother, was appointed as guardian over us. And so, there we were, all ten of us living on our little farm, which was not a farm now but just a house, a big empty barn and lots of land.

Again, here I must say that these are my memories and not those of my brothers and sisters. To them it must have been terribly frightening, with the responsibility of the home and us young ones. They tell me they all just sat for days not knowing what to do, but they must have snapped out of it at some point, for Bernard went back to work in the forest cutting timber, Irving went to the saw mill or cutting timber, Harold continued his job as a busboy, Lottie acquired work in the town, and Everett, who must have been in his early teens, quit school and found part-time work in the town, mowing lawns, gardening, carrying water for the store owners and whatever else he could get. Though the wages he received were very small, perhaps twenty-five cents a day or less, Everett brought home all he could get in food for the family.

Guy at the time was staying with our aunt, two houses up the road. Aunt Gertrude, who had no children, had

*Irving cutting
Albert's hair*

*Frank Cromwell (Papa),
Christie's father*

asked Mamma if one of the boys could stay with her, and though Guy was always at our house to lend a helping hand, he would go up to Aunt Gert's at night. This left the four of us at home during the day: Mae, Theta, Frankie and me, and Guy part of the time. Now this may sound strange but, to Frankie and me, it started to become a very happy life. We grew accustomed to the situation. After all, we had so many big brothers and sisters to care for us and we also had, as we saw it, "the biggest playground in the world." There were lots of fruit trees and berry fields with a variety of berries, lots of places to run and jump and hide, brooks to drink from with stones to jump over, lots of trees deep in the forest where we could go exploring and see, now and then, a deer, or rabbit or woodchuck, owl, squirrel, skunk, beaver and many types of birds. We could be in the woods for hours and not be too hungry for we would feast on apples or berries.

I thought Frankie was the bravest boy in the world and was not afraid of anything, but I was afraid of everything. Crawling things such as caterpillars would make me go screaming to Frankie, who would get rid of whatever it was. Then away we would go, with him walking in front to chase away anything that might frighten me. I can see him now stumbling and waddling along, so clumsy that he would fall every now and again. He was short and stocky and always clumsy, so he stumbled and fell over everything. Then he would scramble up again, brush himself off and say, "Gumma Griddy?" which meant, "Coming Christie?" Sometimes he would jump on something on the ground and tell me to get back. He then would pick up a snake he was standing on until I got past it, and he would let it go unharmed. And so we went through bushes, briers, thistle and swamp... over large boulders, scrambling over brooks, jumping from stone to stone, stooping down to lie on the ground to take a drink from a clear running stream, and then up again to run through trees and bushes. Frankie would be leading me on from one place to another, with me trailing close behind. Often a branch would slap back and swat me across the face, and Frankie would look back and say, "You okay, Griddy?" — trying not to laugh. On seeing that I was all right he would saunter on, "Gumma Griddy," "Come on Christie."

I can recall on one occasion, as I was standing on a large rock watching as Frankie climbed up an apple tree to shake down some of the delicious apples, something in the corner of my eye made me look down, and there right under the rock were two of the largest snakes I had ever seen! They were moving along very slowly, very close together, each going in the opposite direction. So on each end was a large flat head. They were black with yellow, green, and orange stripes. This was the most frightening thing I had ever experienced. It just seemed to paralyze me, I was frozen to the spot there on that rock. Then I could feel myself falling — I was falling right down on those awful snakes and had no power to stop myself.

Everything seemed to be in slow motion, down, down I seemed to fall toward the most frightening thing in the world to me. Suddenly, I felt Frankie grab me and pull me back, "Gee wiz, Griddy, you were falling right on them."

Though Frankie was very young, he had very responsible jobs. He had to help to gather firewood and water from the well, clean up the yard and do many chores around the house. On our trips through our fields, pasture and woods, Frankie always took a saw and axe with him, and was always searching for small trees to cut down, or dry fallen trees. He would cut and chop until he had a good load. Then we would carry or drag home all we could. Frankie usually had his older brothers to help him with all the work but this was not always the case.

And yes, there was a dog; there had always bean a dog in our home. I think Harold always brought them. I have been told about Tuny, Caesar and Chilly, a brown and white mutt who followed us everywhere. Frankie would hitch Chilly up to a sled or old cart, and Chilly would happily pull anything, even a load of wood with me hanging on the back. Old Chilly would try and run through snow, thicket, mud puddles and all, a-panting and going with a dog smile on his face. Chilly was a faithful and loving pet. The greatest fun was to hide from him and have him find us. In the winter, when the snow was very deep, we would build a snow-house, bury ourselves deep inside so we could not be seen, make a small hole in the top, and then call to Chilly. He would come running and dig and scratch fiercely until he uncovered us, his tail wagging and with his big doggie smile he would greet us with big doggie kisses. Yes! To my way of thinking, dogs can smile. Chilly was a very good watchdog too. On one occasion when Mae, Theta, Frankie and I were home alone very late in the night, someone came and started banging on our front door. There came a man's voice. "Let me in," he demanded. He continued banging and pushing on the door trying to force his way in. We were all very afraid. Because Frankie had taught Chilly to be quiet and not bark at times like this, Chilly was growling very deep in his throat and straining to go out after whoever it was. Mae kept telling us all to be quiet. "Perhaps it is someone we know." But as this man went on grumbling and mumbling at the door Frankie said, "Come on Mae, let me set Chilly on him." Mae gave a nod to Frankie and he let go of Chilly. Well that dog was out the door and in no time we heard the man let out one yell and take off running down the road. Minutes later Chilly came back with a piece of the man's pants in his mouth, looking very proud. We learned later that the man was old Frankie Jackson (who was a little confused). He had been up the road visiting with friends, had a little too much to drink and thought he was at his own house.

Though Frankie got help from the older brothers when they were at home, he had the responsibility of getting the chores done. I, at the same time, was to help with the housework, but whenever I got the chance, I was off with Frankie. We explored through the orchards and pastures and deep into the forest where there were tall evergreen trees. We discovered large spruce trees standing about six feet apart, so that when we stood between them it was as if we were in a little room and could not see out through the heavy hanging branches. On the ground were spruce spills and moss, making us comfortable beds. Neither rain nor snow could penetrate through the large bows that shaded the top, with all the branches woven together. One could not see the sky in this comfortable haven. We would stretch out on the soft bed of moss and eat berries or fruit we had gathered, and talk. Frankie would tell me stories about Papa and Mamma. Or we would just listen quietly to the bird sounds. We had learned to identify most of the sounds of the forest. Here we could be alone and at peace. It seemed we were alone in the world — no one could harm us, see us or interrupt our thoughts. Lying flat on our backs looking up at the sky was another wonderful pastime. A time to dream and wonder. Why... Why did Mamma die?

Soon our relatives will come and visit us from Boston and bring us lots of goodies. They did come visiting when Papa and Mamma were alive and they came bringing with them our cousins Lenora, Alice and Kenny. I disliked them right away for they said I was wearing their old clothes. This was true. The pretty panties I had on had came from the barrel that had been sent by Aunt Barbara, their mother, but them saying so hurt my feelings, so I didn't even try to like them. Frankie was not happy with Kenny either, and when Lottie insisted that Frankie take Kenny with him to pick berries, Frankie was really upset.

Kenny was so curious, wanting to know everything. "What is this, what is that? Can I have that to take back to Boston with me?" Frankie was so tired of his many questions that when he pointed up a tree and said, "Oh what is that? Can I have it? I'd like to take that back home with me," Frankie looked and saw that it was a hornet's nest and said, "Yes you can have it. Go up the tree and get it." Frankie knew what would happen. He had his path all picked out. As Kenny climbed up the tree and Frankie saw him pluck the hornet's nest off the tree branch and start down with a big grin, so happy to have his prize, Frankie took off running. Glancing back he could see hornets all coming out and starting to circle around Kenny's head. Arriving home first, Frankie just went and sat in the yard. Then he heard Kenny right behind, screaming and bawling and being followed by hornets, his head and face covered with many bites that were already starting to swell. Kenny never asked to go with Frankie again.

Just up in the pasture was a large tree, which could be seen from the upstairs window. This tree had scratches on it, bear tracks all around it, fur on the tree and the scent of the animal often present. Our brothers had often spoken of sensing its presence, even hearing it breathing. They came to realize the bear was not there to harm them, but seemed to have made its home there in our pasture. Irving said after a time it seemed the bear was like part of the family. We often peeped out of the window at the tree, and if the bear was there, we could see the tree shaking. So off we would run to see if we could catch the bear there, or at least get to see it. I, of course, would run a little behind, afraid that the bear really would be there.

One evening we were walking through the pasture quite late. (We had stayed later than usual in the forest and it had grown dark.) As we got to the pasture, we heard a growling sound. Now I am ready to run and our dog Chilly gave a low growl and started toward the sound. He was made to stay by a strict command from Frankie. Chilly was taught to be quiet and not to bark, so he would growl low in his throat. So now he was crouching with his tail between his legs, his hair standing up on his back, staring into the thicket. Warning Chilly and me to be quiet, Frankie stood very still. "There is nothing to be afraid of," Frankie said, "just someone trying to frighten us. Let's just keep walking." And so we went on, with me hanging onto Frankie's raggedy jacket sleeve. Frankie started to mimic the sound, making a growling sound. All the way out of the pasture and through the orchard the growling continued to follow, with Frankie continuing to mimic. By now I too started to believe someone was playing tricks on us. When we arrived home and told Bernard of the sound we had heard, he was quite upset with us and warned us about staying too late in the woods. "Bears are hungry at this time of the year. They may also have cubs they are protecting so stay out of the woods after dark." The next day Uncle Roy told Frankie that Walter Cosman had spotted a bear in his woods, which was just next to our land.

We forgot all about that incident and the warning from Bernard, as we always did. One frightening experience did not stop us from exploring, so again we are strolling home, it is growing dark, and suddenly Frankie grabs my arm and says, "Stop, listen," and we can hear scratching. "It's coming from the bear tree," Frankie whispered. Commanding Chilly to be quiet, we crept slowly along. Then Frankie stepped forward a few paces and very slowly parted some branches, and there at the bear tree stood the bear, standing on its two back paws. Its front paws were up onto the trunk of the tree. It was scratching and now and again stopped and started licking something. It was so engrossed in what it was doing that it did not seem to notice us, but went on scratching and licking. I don't know about Frankie or Chilly, but I was too frightened to move. As we stood staring at the bear, it turned its head and sniffed the air, then slowly put its paws down and disappeared into the thicket, leaving Frankie and me wide-eyed and shocked.

We had seen that old bear. We continued home saying, "Just wait until we tell them fellows we saw the bear." But we had been told not to stay in the woods after dark, and they would be all upset and scolding us, talking on and on about the dangers of being in the woods after dark. So we kept quiet about it, and when we were in our secret place, in the forest, under the spruce trees, we talked about our seeing that old bear.

We always tried to do as Lottie told us, for she would get so upset with us if we misbehaved. She was so soft-hearted that rather than giving us a good spanking when we did wrong she would look all upset as if she was about to cry and say, "You fellows know better than that! Why did you do that?" She would make us feel very bad and sorry we had messed up. This was unlike Mae, who would give us a well-deserved cuff upside the head. But Lottie should not have asked us to keep Aunt Girlie's hens out of the porch...

Aunt Girlie and Uncle Roy's property was just next to ours, and there was no fence between, so their animals were free to come and go wherever they pleased, and their hens just could not stay out of our porch. Those darn hens were always coming into our porch and leaving their droppings. We tried everything to keep them out, but nothing worked.

Now Frankie had a lash whip he had made out of rawhide. His brothers had taught him how to use it very well. The porch had two doors — one led to the yard the other to the side of the house — and two windows. Frankie's plan was for me to stand in one door and him in the other with the lash whip, "Now don't let them get past you Griddy. Just chase them over to me and I will lash them with my whip. That should keep them out. They will be afraid to come in the porch again." Well, it was not long before twenty or more of them were all in the porch. I crept quietly and stood in the side door, with Frankie in the other. The hens started getting excited seeing they were trapped. They began to cackle and run all around looking for a place to escape. Some jumped over my head, some landing in my hair, feathers flying all over my face. Some flew out of the window. All were cackling and fluttering. I was shooing them off and chasing them towards Frankie, who was lashing out at them with his whip. Finally all the hens escaped out of the porch except a big saucy one who was ready to fly into Frankie's face. Frankie lashed out at this sassy hen and the whip twirled around the hen's neck, tied into a knot and stayed around its neck.

Frankie tugged at it, and the whip would not untie, and now the hen starts walking very slowly out of the porch with Frankie holding onto the whip, now and then giving a little tug but the whip would not untie. The hen was making a strange sound as it waddled slowly along — gulp-glunk-gulp-glunk... As it walked its feet were crossing over, like a drunken man. Away it went, slowly walking towards home. This hen was going home with Frankie's lash whip around its neck and Frankie walking slowly behind, giving a little tug at the whip now and then. Me? I'm no good! I am on the ground laughing. And away they went, the hen going gulp-glunk-gulp-glunk, and Frankie tug-tug-tugging. Just before the hen reached home, the whip finally dropped off, and Frankie was able to retrieve it. I was rolling on the ground laughing.

The next time we went up to Aunt Girlie's she said, "I wonder what happened to that hen?" And when we looked, we saw that the hen had not one feather around its neck. "It's losing its feathers and I don't know why," said Aunt Girlie. Well, we had to stand there and pretend not to know what had happened, until we were able to get away, and then we fell about, laughing our heads off.

There were many little incidences like that and problems we would get into, which we even talk about to this day and have lots of laughs over. Like the time we were throwing rocks trying to hit the top of the barn. Frankie's rock went too far and we heard Uncle Roy say, "Ouch. Who's throwing rocks?" We did not know he was working in his garden, just behind our barn.

We loved going up to Aunt Girlie's, for their house was on a hill and it was great to dash down the hill to home. However, this was a tricky run for there were sharp stones there, and many times we stubbed our toe on one and went flying, then sat on the ground crying, rubbed mud on the spot and went running on. We had made a path through the stone wall that ran through between the properties, and there were beautiful wild roses that had grown on the wall. Though they had sharp thorns, the roses were lovely and had a wonderful scent. Once, when coming out of Aunt Girlie's, both of us starting to run and Frankie hit a rock and went flying, landing right in the middle of the rose bush. He went right out of sight in the roses. "Frankie! You all right?" I called. Then Frankie came crawling out of the rose bushes, picking thorns out of his arms and legs, rose buds and petals flying all around him. Without even looking at me he said, "Okay Griddy, you can laugh now."

My childhood is one I would not change for the world; those were the best years of my life. The most outstanding times being Christmas.

It was Christmas Eve, the sun had gone down, we were still sawing and splitting wood, making sure we had enough to last over Christmas. We were talking about what we wanted for Christmas. I looked up and I swear I saw Santa Claus and his reindeers go past the moon. There was another occasion when we were walking through the woods and heard what sounded like a very loud meow. I immediately ran away just knowing it had to be a wildcat and grabbed Frankie as always; but again Frankie made Chilly and me be still as he stood peering through the bushes. Soon, out popped a scruffy looking cat, followed by five little kittens, all meowing at the same time, making it sound like one big cat. The mother cat was so weak and sick she seemed to have just given up and come to us for help. It was not long before we had all the kittens and their mother at home warm and fed — Blocky, Graylegs, Mayonnaise, Pugtail and Stripes. The mother did not live long but we think she was happy that she had found a home for her kittens.

There were some days we were so hungry our stomachs would pain — we called them hungry days. Those were the days we had nothing to eat until evening, when Lottie would come home with food and prepare a great supper. I would be as hungry as the rest but when we would sit down to eat, I would get sick to my stomach. No one knew at the time I was suffering from a blood disorder, which I am now being treated for, but my being too sick to eat mattered not to Theta and Frankie. I can still hear them now. "Lottie, Christie doesn't want hers. Can we have it?"

This was, I now realize, a very bad time for my sisters and brothers. Their decision for us to stay together was a great thing, but it takes a lot to feed a large family, and in those days, wages were very small. A foreman at the sawmill received three dollars a day; workers got one dollar a day; housecleaning paid twenty-five cents a day. The offer from the people of the village of Weymouth Falls to take us into their homes and care for us was a sensible solution. After all, the families in our village were no better off than we were, and most had large families. I personally feel their offer was a very thoughtful one, for added mouths to feed would be a burden to any of the relatives or families in that small village.

Why do I always love Christmas and the pretence of Santa Claus? Well, perhaps it is because of brother Bernard, who, to me, became a big, strong, stern father, who, when he spoke, we jumped. He did not have to beat us, but we just knew we had better behave when he was at home. He was only at home some weekends. He came with a big knapsack on his back, just packed with food and items for the home, almost always a treat for us young ones — peanuts or candy. To me he always looked angry and would always say, "This house looks like a Hoorays nest." We did not know what a Hooray was but it must have kept a messy nest. And we would rush and start cleaning up even though we had thought the house looked pretty good. After all, we had cleaned it up for the weekend, but to Bernard it looked like a Hooray's nest. And the question was always. "Were you fellows hungry, did you have enough to eat?" We always told him that we had lots to eat, though we had had some hungry days, because we all knew how upset he would get and we did not want to see the look of utter despair on his face. Then he would stomp up the stairs and we could hear him talking to himself. Then soon he would come running down the stairs singing and be ready to joke and kid with us. I was always afraid of Bernard when he had his serious face on. But when he was relaxing and talking with the others, I would creep closer until I was leaning on his big arm or swinging between his legs. He was big and strong, with great bulging muscles, and I liked his woodsy smell, mixed with shaving cream.

Frankie thought Bernard was everything in the world and likewise Bernard loved his baby brother and would take him with him everywhere he went. This was very upsetting to me for I was accustomed to going everywhere with Frankie. I was always told to stay with my sisters, not understanding that Bernard wanted time with his brother, and me being a girl would just not be comfortable with their man-talk. So I would stand and watch them walking off together and think, "Bernard doesn't like me."

Perhaps I love Christmas because of Irving — short, stocky, always with a nice smile. When he was at home he would sit by the corner of the old wood stove, mending his clothes, repairing his boots or darning his socks. Mamma must have taught him these things and would be doing them for him if she were there. I was told that Irving was a Mamma's boy and sort of spoiled by her. But now he was on his own... When he would sit repairing his stuff, Frankie and I would get as near to him as we could, for we knew that sooner or later he would start telling us of a movie he had seen or of something that had happened to him when at work, or some time during the work week. He could tell a story and make it so real you felt as if you were right there. We would sit very quietly, taking in every word, sometimes sharing a treat we had received from one of them. We did not always get treats, only if they could afford them, so whenever we did we were so excited and would sit very close together on the old wooden lounge and share every drop.

There always stays in my memory those terrible lice! Yes, we got lice (I suppose every school has a problem with lice at some time), even though our older sisters made sure we kept ourselves clean. Lottie and Mae always stressed the importance of washing our hair and skin, and making sure we had clean clothing every day. We still got lice in our hair, and to add to this there developed a sort of fungus called scabies, awful sores which were full of pus. The lice would mingle with the pus, so there was pain along with the itch, and we thought we would go crazy with this terrible condition. We tried everything to rid ourselves of these lice and scabies. Then Irving came home in the middle of the week: this never happened, Irving never came home during the week. We wondered why he was home today. Well, we soon found out! Irving carried a bag in his hand and he went to the stove with the scrub bucket, which he filled with hot water, and saying nothing to Theta and me, called Frankie, "Come on upstairs, Frankie." He must have a special treat for Frankie we thought and went on with whatever we were doing. It was not long before we heard Frankie howling and moaning as if in great pain. We wondered what Irving was torturing him with, or perhaps Frankie had done something real bad and was being punished, but what? Theta and I just sat there not knowing what to do. Then all the crying stopped, all was quiet for a time, and then Frankie came down the stairs looking as if he had been through a great cleaning machine. His head was wrapped up like a mummy. Irving followed and, getting another bucket of hot water, he said, "Come on, Theta." He took her by the arm and, very reluctantly, she went along. Soon the same sounds of protest were coming from upstairs, though Theta was making sounds of anger rather than admit to being hurt by her big brother. I was the last to go. Arriving in the bedroom shared by half the boys, I could smell a very strange odour. The bucket of hot water was sitting by Irving's bed. Irving sat on the bed, pulled me down and holding me very firmly with his knees he started shaking some strong-smelling powder on my head. Suddenly my head began to burn and sting like many bees were stinging me, and, with a fine comb, Irving was combing through my hair.

Now I am screaming and kicking and fighting to get away from this awful burn, but try as I may I could not get out of Irving's tight grip. Now he was pouring some dark brown liquid over my head and this added a new and different burn — adding pain to the sting of the scabs that had formed on our heads. Next Irving dipped my head in the hot water and I felt I would choke from the smell, steam and discomfort of it all. Then suddenly it all stopped...

Everything that was itching, burning or stinging went away and now there was a warm, soothing feeling all over my head. Irving then dried me off with a warm towel, wrapped my head in a nice clean cloth and sent me downstairs where Theta and Frankie sat by the stove. I joined them and so there we sat, three quiet mummies. The pain was gone. The sting was gone. The itch was gone. And the scabs were gone. Best of all — the lice were gone. No more lice! Thanks to Irving.

Irving was to me a very handsome man with a light brown complexion and curly black hair like we all had. Our hair is like Papa's, black and curly. When he was expressing himself or telling us a story, Irving's eyebrows would arch up and down, or one eyebrow would shoot up and the other one down. His expressions were great to watch. Irving loved music and had a mouth organ he could play beautifully. He came home with a guitar one day, and it wasn't long before he and most of us learned to play it. When he left to join the army, he gave his guitar to Theta.

Harold was Santa Claus to me — the brother who worked at the Goodwin Hotel as a busboy. He would mostly come home on Sunday afternoons. He had a bike and would come riding swiftly up the road. Rushing into the house all wide-eyed and out of breath as if he was being chased by something or someone, he'd start telling us a story. Sometimes he would tell of a dog chasing a cat and nearly running into him causing his bike to go one way and him the other. He made his stories so funny, all the family would be laughing at his comics. Though he did not get a great wage as a busboy, Harold was a great support to the family, especially at Christmas. On Christmas Eve, he would come rushing into the house (as always, in a hurry) all big-eyed and begin to warn us against touching or looking into the large cartons he had carried in. He was always loaded down with gifts for all. We would not think of peeking into his private cartons, for we did not wish to spoil his surprise. On Christmas Day Harold was the silliest and the one most likely to be found on the floor playing with our toys. Whenever I think of Harold, I start to laugh as some memory of his silly antics comes to mind.

We (most of the family) could dance, which we try to do to this day. When we all get together we often try to strike a step but none of us could do as well as Harold. He danced like the professional dancers. One great thing I remember is on some days as we walked down the road from school, Harold would sometimes ride by on his bike and almost always give us a handful of change, some money or a candy bar. Harold was, and is, a great artist. I recall he used to get me to stand on the kitchen lounge so he could draw me. I was always amazed at how well he could capture my likeness. He has continued his artwork, and his paintings are known in many parts of the world.

Everett really meant Christmas to me. He, as I said before, was the one who lit the fire in the morning on Christmas Day, who always pretended there was nothing under the Christmas tree for us. He was a very quiet person who would be found sitting in the evening in front of the stove, his chair leaning back on two legs, sound asleep. He certainly needed the rest after a hard day's work, perhaps mowing lawns or weeding someone's garden, then helping Frankie with the work at home. It never seemed to bother him when we, Theta, Frankie and I, would cuddle near him or play tricks on him. We got great fun when we would quietly pile sticks of firewood on him, or shoes, anything we could get on him without waking him up, and when he did awake and start to get up everything would drop off. This we hoped would frighten him, but he would only laugh and chase us, and when caught we would get some real sound slaps, though never hard enough to hurt too badly. He never became angry with us, no matter what we did.

They tell me that when I was just starting to walk all the older ones would sit and say, "Come here Christie," and I would always go straight to Everett. I was always happy wrapped in Everett's arms. Everett received very small wages — about twenty-five cents a day — and whatever he got, he spent on food for us, keeping nothing for himself. He was a very tall, slim handsome young man who should have been in school — the young girls were all crazy about him. One of the ladies he worked for, Mrs. Grearson, would fill a brown paper bag full of goodies — cookies, doughnuts, muffins and many other lovely treats. On the day he worked for Mrs. Grearson, we young ones would all wait for Everett to come home, and when he would pop in sight, we all ran to meet him. He would throw his head back laughing, then run backwards trying to get away from us all rushing at him. At first he would pretend to keep the nice full greasy bag of goodies from us, but then he would give it to us. What a feast we would have! Everett kept nothing for himself.

Our niece Joyce (Aunt Girlie's daughter), who lived up on the hill and was always at our house, remembers the treats, and whenever we all get together for a family reunion, always reminds us of the Grearson bag, for she had shared in the eating of the goodies in that greasy bag.

Guy... I can't say enough about him. Guy was a mainstay in all my life. But here I can only tell you of him as a boy. He was not a constant person in my life for he stayed with Aunt Gertrude, who lived just two houses up the road. Her house was just past Aunt Girlie's gate, past the bushes and the little bridge where the mint leaves grew. We could smell the mint whenever we crossed the bridge. Aunt Gert, as we called her, had no children and had asked Mamma if one of the boys could stay with her. I don't know why Guy was picked. All I knew was that Guy was always at home in the daytime, helping with all the work like all the rest but come evening, Guy would go up to Aunt Gert's. He loved to laugh like all of us but had a very bad temper and would fly off the handle at any given moment. If he was not in the mood to play we knew to leave him alone. We were all aware of how quickly he would become angry so we, or I should say I, was careful not to anger him. I did not really get to know Guy until much later; therefore, I will save my opinion of Guy until later.

Now going on to Lottie... I wanted to cover the five older brothers first and now my three sisters, the oldest being Lottie. From my earliest memory of Christmas, Lottie was the one who trimmed the house for the occasion. She was working in Halifax as I remember and had mentioned in one of her many letters to Mamma not to trim the tree, that she was bringing with her all the trimmings. This was my earliest memory of Christmas. I recall sitting watching as Lottie hung the most beautiful bulbs on the tree. I also remember her sitting talking to Mamma with her arm around me, showing me love in a quiet way. She seemed so different from the three of us... Mae, Theta and me... very lady-like, even in her speech. I hoped to grow up and be like her. Now Lottie had to be the mother, and what a mother she was! She was very strict, and when we would misbehave (and we were always misbehaving), she would get very upset and hurt and look as if she was about to cry, "Why did you fellows have to do that? You know better than that!" She would go on and on and be so disappointed with us. It would make me feel so awful I would wish she would just give us a good beating, it would not have hurt as much as her look of utter disgust and disappointment.

The one thing Frankie and I hated to do was to go up the

road to the one-room schoolhouse. Oh, it was fine when the older ones of the family were going, but when it came down to just Frankie and me, we hated it! I was a shy person. They said I was bashful. I was too shy to talk to people and kept my head down the entire time, so I could not make friends easily. I would sit at my desk at school and think of everything except what we were supposed to be learning. My mind would wonder off, thinking of home or music, singing a song that would be going around in my head, just going quietly into another world, not at school, but wishing to be running through the fields. I also can remember when the children called us names, they said we were bastards. I didn't know what the word meant at the time but I gathered it had to do with us having no parents. But we knew we were orphans. Why did they call us this other name and in a manner like it was a dirty word? Sometimes they refused to take my hand in a game of play, whispering "bastard" or "lost cause," and then laugh amongst themselves. At those times I would stand alone in the schoolyard and think of where I would rather be.

Frankie was very quick to make friends. He wanted only to be friendly to everyone and he did not like to fight. I don't think he was cowardly but just loved everyone and wanted to have friends, and did not understand why the other boys would want to pick on him. Frankie just loved people and often went up the road visiting the people there even though they were not all related to us. He would visit, talk and listen to all the stories. The old folk would tell him of their lives in the old days. The older folk liked Frankie just like they had our father and often said, "He is just like his father Frankie."

The teachers were quite nice on the whole except one male teacher who just seemed to love using the strap and at the end of each day when he was teaching, Frankie got the strap because he did not finish his work. I can see him now walking up slowly with his work paper shaking in his hand. He carried his head on one side when he was confused or frightened for he knew what he would get when old Rylen Walton saw his work was not finished. "Hold them out properly," I would hear him say as Frankie gingerly put up his hands. And the strap would come down on his hands... the hands that were so important to me... the hands that held mine as we ran... the hands that would give me most of his candy... the hands that lashed out with his whip at anything that frightened me and that comforted me when I cried. And now these hands would be hurt and turning red. Frankie tried not to cry then but he and I would cry together on our way home.

This went on until a new teacher came... Penelope Anderson, daughter of the Rev. Anderson, who preached at the Baptist Church in Weymouth Falls. Penelope was pretty and tall with a soft voice, and she paid strict attention to all the students. If you did not understand your work, she took the time to explain, sitting beside you and talking in her quiet voice until you understood. It did not take long for her to notice that Frankie was having problems. One day she went and sat with him and soon discovered that Frankie was having trouble seeing the blackboard — the

Penelope Anderson with her students in Weymouth Falls, mid-1930s, Christie is the first on the left in the middle row.

reason he was not able to finish his work. So, the previous teacher was strapping him for something that Frankie could not prevent. Penelope Anderson, this lovely person who paid attention to her students and could see that Frankie needed help, sent a note home to Lottie telling her Frankie needed to go to see about his eyes, perhaps needed glasses. She was my favourite teacher, and to this day, when I visit her, I still call her teacher. She did not stay long at the school in Weymouth Falls; she went on to bigger and better employment in Ontario. We all missed her when she left.

There was one boy at school who was always a friend to Frankie and would stop the others from picking on him — Albert Cromwell, a distant cousin of ours. He, his brothers and other boys often came down to play with Frankie, even though they were told to stay away from our place. I could not stand Albert, just hated "old big-head Albert," as I called him. He was always teasing and pretending to put caterpillars on me knowing how frightened I was of any worms. Many times when we would be in the woods gathering firewood, old big-head Albert would show up, sometimes with his father's ox team, to help carry home the load of wood. Frankie would be so happy to see him. He would cut down much larger trees than Frankie could, showing off because he had big muscles. Then, loading them on his ox team he would carry them home for Frankie, even though when his father found out he had taken the ox team out, he would get a good whipping. Old big-head Albert would continue to do this again and again. But to me he was interrupting our fun; it was much better with just Frankie, Chilly the dog and me.

Ours was a one-room school with a wood stove in the front for heating the place. We children gathered around it in winter when it was cold. The big boys used to help gather wood to keep the fire going. There were two outhouses, one for girls and one for boys; two cloakrooms at each entrance, one for girls, the other for the boys. This being the only school in Weymouth Falls, it housed all the children — from primer-class to grade eight. High school was in the town of Weymouth.

At the end of the day I would always wait at the boys' cloakroom door for Frankie and we would walk home together hand in hand. They laughed at us because of this and many other things and now that I am older I can understand why they thought us pretty strange. Other brothers and sisters were not that close and did not usually act like that, but I think we were relying on each other, holding onto each other. We had lost so much we did not want to lose each other.

So one day I stood outside waiting for Frankie to come out and I could hear lots of noise inside. Going in to investigate I found the room was jammed with all the children who were looking on. When they saw me trying to jam in, they were all quick to say, "Maxine is beating up Frankie!" The mention of Maxine's name sent chills up my spine. She was one of the toughest girls in school, she could whip anyone in school and when she was called up to the front for a strapping the school became deathly quiet for we all knew we were in for a show. She would kick, bite and scratch when the teacher tried to strap her. Once, when she was fighting with another girl, she knocked the girl's tooth out with one blow. She fought like a man and we all stayed away from her. I had no reason to dislike Maxine but now if she was hurting my brother I would have to do something. But I could not understand why she was fighting with Frankie. He had told me of some of the girls he liked and Maxine was one of them. Frankie had a big crush on Sylvia, Loretta, Leona and many girls. We talked often of who we liked and disliked in school. So what was this all about, I asked myself. When I had finally pushed through the crowd enough to see what was happening, Frankie was not fighting with Maxine at all but was holding up his hands trying to ward off the blows she was throwing at him. She was hitting and kicking at him with all her strength. Frankie was just trying to keep her from hitting and scratching him. I knew Frankie would not fight with a girl. He was also crying because the crowd was laughing at him for being beat up by a girl. They were all screaming and taunting Maxine on to beat Frankie up.

Well, I don't know if I walked or flew through the air; I only know I found myself in Maxine's face, my fist smashing into her pretty face. I can't remember us falling down but I know I was on top of her, hitting and hitting, then being pulled off by the teacher. I don't know if I won that fight, I only know I saw red, and anger like a grate-burning fire came over me. I walked over, took Frankie by the hand and we went, running as always, home. That was the only time I fought at school — I was too quiet and shy. I was told later that Maxine was angry with Frankie because she liked him and Frankie was talking to another girl. I do not know all the facts and don't really wish to know, but the fight was about Frankie and the girls who liked him and I can see why, for Frankie was a cute boy with deep dimples in his cheeks, pretty curls, long eyelashes. He looked more like a pretty girl than a boy, and I often wished I looked more like him instead of this skinny plain crane of a girl.

How I wished I was like Mae and Theta, who were so outgoing and friendly to everyone and had many friends. I just could not make myself talk and come out of myself though I so wanted to be friendly. I was only talkative when I was at home and only happy when at home and in the woods or fields with Frankie. We ran most of the time through our fields and the fields of our neighbours. Our house was directly on the line that separated the White people's area from that of the coloured district, as it was called. The house just down the road from ours was the home of the late Mr. Charles McDonald, who had passed away but had been a friend of the family as far as I can tell from the stories I hear from my siblings. Now his family had come to live on the property.

Mrs. Hope Langdale (who had five or six grown children and grandchildren and many family members) and her family were very friendly. We played with their children, went to their homes, and they came to ours. Mrs. Langdale had a cow and would sell Frankie milk, and if Frankie did not have the money, she would just give it to him. The next farmhouse down the road from them belonged to Mr. and Mrs. Cosman, who were just as friendly. Often we played with their children in their barn, jumping from the hayloft into a pile of hay. They had a large farm with lots of fruit trees and strawberry fields, and would allow us to go and pick their apples or anything as long as we did not run through the wheat fields and trample down the wheat. So, we always walked around the edge of the wheat fields. They also had a pond that they allowed us to skate on during the winter. None of these White people seemed to be prejudiced, or perhaps they were and had shown it to others, but to Frankie and me they were just people that looked different. They had straight hair, where ours was curly; their hair was brown, yellow or red, and looked like rope or horse tails; their eyes were blue or green. But that mattered not, they were all good friends, and like the relatives and friends in the coloured district, they were always giving us something nice to eat whenever we went there, or would even call us in to get treats of pastry, fruit or drink. My only feeling of envy came because there always seemed to be lots of delicious-looking food in their kitchens, and their children would walk away from the table leaving food on their plates. Now, this we would never do for we never ever had enough. We lapped up everything we got!

There was one mean old White man, old Fred John, who had a shack just across from the Cosman's and who also had land and fruit trees and berry fields but would not allow anyone to go near his property. He owned a lovely home in the town but also owned this property. He was always there in his shack or working on his land. There were lots of delicious apples on his trees and we just loved to get in there and steal his apples. After all, they tasted much better when we stole them. He also had large yummy strawberries. Now if, by chance, old Fred John was not in his shack we would just go and help ourselves, but not if he was there (and we would know that he was for we could see the smoke coming from his chimney). We often saw him walking around his property, mostly carrying a hunting rifle under his arm. It was said that he filled the gun with course salt and would shoot at you. The salt was harmless but gave an awful sting.

So when Theta would say, "Let's go down and get some apples from Fred John," we would get very excited for we knew this would be lots of fun. Wearing very large clothing with lots of pockets, we would walk casually down the road and, as we grew near his shack, we would call, "Mr. John? Mr. John?" After some time, and us calling many times, he would come out. His big red face with an angry look would cause Frankie and me to start to run, but Theta would hold us there and say in a very sweet voice. "Please can we have some of those apples over there in your orchard?" He would look at us as if we were crazy and say very gruffly, "Apples? What apples?" "Those apples there in your orchard," Theta would repeat in her sweetest voice. "No!" he would answer, and then disappear into his shack.

By now, Frankie and I would have run back up the road a few feet. Theta would turn, walk slowly back to us, and we would walk back up the road as if we were very hurt and were going home. When we were sure we were out of sight of old mean Fred John, we would quickly dash to the side of the road and into the bushes. Soon we would be in the orchard and now sneaking slowly along, bending down low through the grass, we would rush to his trees and Frankie would be up the tree in no time, shaking down the apples, and Theta and I would be gathering them up and stuffing our many pockets. Sometimes we would see him coming, first his big straw hat, then his red face, bowed legs and then the gun. Too late to run, we would lay down real flat in the grass until he passed. He would stand looking here and there, as if he knew we were there, then he would go on through his field.

Once Frankie got caught up the tree. Theta and I were running away, and looking back, we noticed Frankie was not with us. We saw him still up the tree and Fred John walking right under. We ducked behind a stone wall, watched and waited. Fred John walked around under the tree; we hoped he wouldn't look up, Frankie told us afterwards that he had been so afraid an apple would fall. As Fred John walked away grumbling to himself, Frankie slid slowly down the tree, then ran as fast as he could. We only stole his apples because he was so mean and would rather let his apples rot than let us have them.

It was not always Fred John who chased us off his land. We could be happily picking his strawberries, not looking for Mr. John for we would have checked and found him not around, so we would be relaxed, picking away, when we would hear a big snort. Looking up we would see a big black bull watching us, snorting and frothing at the mouth. This was a very cross bull (everyone knew Mr. John had a very cross bull), who was now about to charge us, for he was pawing the ground. Now this meant only one thing... run! We would get out of there as fast as our legs could carry us — grass and strawberries flying! Grabbing at each other, we ran, just missing the flowertops, buttercups, dandelions and daisies, being loped off and sticking between our toes. Now and again, one of us would stub our toe and go flying. The other two would stop to help the other up and off we would run, too afraid to look back, all getting over the fence just in time before the bull's horns struck. Then he would stand there shaking his head and clawing the ground. This was, to us, the greatest fun and we would laugh at ourselves all the way home.

Frankie and I loved it when we could go up the road to the homes of our uncles and aunts. There were lots of them — relatives of our mother's, sisters and brothers of our grandmother (so they were our great aunts and uncles). They seemed very old to us, had strange habits and ways of speaking, and seemed very old fashioned in their thinking, We loved them all and when we were asked to go on an errand to their homes we ran off with joy. We welcomed the chance to talk to them and listen to whatever they had to say.

All families in small villages borrowed from each other. Many times we had to borrow oil for the lamps or something like that, so up the hill to Aunt Girlie and Uncle Roy's we would run, "Griddy you- you- you tell her because- I-I-I-I stutter too much," Frankie would say when on our way, for when he got all excited he would stutter. We must first knock at the door (it didn't matter how often we visited anyone, we must knock before entering), and when told to come in we must then stand by the door and not expect to be asked to sit. We were expected to just stand and state our business right away: "Aunt Girlie, Lottie would like to know if you have a little bit of oil to loan us, please?"

Aunt Girlie had a very quick, snappy, sharp voice and her first reply would sometimes be, "I ain't got a bit." Then Uncle Roy might say, "Ah we must have a small drop left in the oil can," and he would drain whatever was left into the bottle we had brought with us. With a big thank you, we would be out the door, down the hill and home with big grins — so proud we had saved the day and gotten oil — enough for the night anyway.

Now if we did not get the oil from the first relative, we would go to the next nearest one. Never would we return home without the oil. It was not that we had to, but we just loved the adventure of trying to get oil, or anything we were sent for. It made us seem helpful and important, needed, and as I said, it was a chance to visit those interesting people. So on we would go, from house to house, never using the road but running through yards, swamps, over fences, through shortcuts, ducking past cross dogs to the next relative.

As we knocked, we would hear Uncle George, "Come in... you're out," and as we walked in, "Well Christie and

Uncle George and Aunt Hattie's house, now abandoned

Frankie... come in, come in and have a seat (sniff-sniff)."
Aunt Hattie, seated in her rocking chair, mending or sewing
something, had sinus trouble and always sniffed. After we
had given our reason for coming she would say, "Yes, we
must have some oil left. George, get the oil can and see if
we can't find some oil for these children (sniff-sniff)." Uncle
George would be sitting in the corner by the big iron stove,
chewing tobacco, looking hard at us as if he was angry,
though we knew him better than that. We would, by now,
be sitting on the comfortable covered lounge by the stove.
Uncle George would spit in his spittoon behind the stove,
then start to tell us some silly remarks or jokes to make us
laugh as he slowly picked himself up from his cozy seat. A
very tall man, wearing bib overalls with one brace down,
the sleeves of his long underwear showing as he walked
across the floor, would strike a step as he sang some tune,
"Everyone welcome to my house. Come after breakfast,
bring along a lunch and leave before suppertime." Then he
would throw his head back and laugh. Aunt Hattie would

always say, "Now George stop telling those children your foolishness (sniff-sniff)," though she too would be shaking with laughter at Uncle George.

Aunt Girt, Uncle George's sister, lived just down the hill from them. She was the lady Guy stayed with. To me, she was so pretty with laughing eyes; her skin (like all the ladies in our family) was a beautiful biscuit brown; she had long hair that she could sit on and would make into a long braid, which she wound up into a large pug at the back of her head; she wore long dresses and there were always two or three layers of different coloured frocks, each one shorter than the other. She, like Uncle George, was always joking and had a large loud laugh. "Child," she would say, as we told what we had come for, "By the time I filled Al's lamp and Guy's lamp and Jackson's lamp (Jackson was a friend who visited sometimes), I had no oil left for my lamp." Then she would laugh that big loud laugh that made her pretty cheeks pop out. I always found myself just staring at her; she was so attractive. She had had one son, who drowned at the age of sixteen.

Aunt Girlie and Aunt Hattie were sisters to my mother's mother, our grandmother, who lived in Boston. They had that lovely biscuit brown skin, something like light brown sugar, pretty black hair and friendly smiles. There was also a brother, Uncle Rodney — Uncle Rod we were told to call him — and what a character! He was always nodding his head when trying to make a point or to show he knew what he was talking about; he was very matter of fact, and what he said was true, don't question him, he knew, and "that was that!" It took forever for him to tell a story for he told everything in such detail. Uncle Rod had a cow that gave very good milk so he sold milk and cream. Many people bought cream from him and when we would pick lots of strawberries and Lottie would make strawberry shortcake, we would be sent up to buy cream from Uncle Rod. "Now, now, now, look who it is! Why it is… let me see now… Yes, this is Frankie (nod-nod), just like his father (nod-nod) and

Mae... no, no, it ain't Mae... Theta... no, it's that one born on Christmas day! (big nod). Yes, they called her Christie... Well come on in, Frankie and Christie." Then turning to his wife, "Look who it is, remember when this child was born? (nod-nod) Christmas morning... they called her Christie, yes... (nod-nod). Have a seat and sit down. Now what did you say your sister Lottie wanted?" Again we start to try, and for the umpteenth time, to make our rehearsed speech: "Lottie would like to buy a pint of whipping cream." "Oh yes, yes, now did you say she wanted it to whip?" (nod) "Yes sir," we would answer. "Yes I will get it right away. You children must be tired and hungry, walking all this way up here," and turning to his wife, "Give these children something to eat (big nod). Now you said your sister wanted it to whip?" (another big nod) "Yes sir," we would answer again.

It did not matter how long it took for us to get Uncle Rod to understand, we had better stay there and answer very politely or we would be in trouble, not only from Uncle Rod, but if Lottie found out we were not polite we would get it.

There were many comical characters living on Weymouth Falls Road. They were so good to us. On cold winter days when it would be snowing and blustering, they would call us in and have us warm ourselves and give us something to eat and a warm drink before going on. We would hope though that Mrs. Dearing would not see us on these days for we were very nearly home by the time we passed her house. We would run all the way past her place to home but if she saw us she would scream, "Frankie and Christie, get in here!" and we would be warmed and fed. We always wondered what size her baking pans were for she would give us the biggest slice of bread we had ever seen.

It is said that it takes a village to raise a child. Well, in our village all the adults had a part in raising us, and if we were caught doing anything wrong by any of the people in Weymouth Falls we were scolded and even given a sting around the legs with a switch, if needed.

Mae recalls one aunt, who whenever she met us on the road would go right to the side of the road and break off a switch from the bushes and chase us. "I saw you, I saw what you did," she would say, "and now you are going to get it." She could run as fast as we could, so run as we might, we would all get a sting from her switch. She never missed one of us. We never knew if she had seen us doing something wrong or not, but we knew when we saw "Aunt Yide" coming, we had better try and get out of her reach for she switched us for just thinking about doing something wrong. And we couldn't ever let any of the old aunts catch us eating the nice juicy blackberries that grew along the roadside. "Don't eat those dirty berries. Take them home and wash them," they would demand, with looks of utter disgust. As soon as they were out of sight, we would go right on eating them. They taste better dirty.

I must say again these are my memories, some may just be my dreams, but to me they all really happened. I can recall Papa sitting me up on the horse, Bob, and me afraid, Frankie and I sitting on the black covered wagon, being driven to town by Papa and Mamma, who spoiled me, and a farm, and a cow named Bessie, and a pig who loved it when I scratched his neck.

So now the home seemed so empty with just the four of us, Mae, Theta, Frankie and me (and Lottie when she was not at work). Lottie had taken to holding me on her lap and rocking me to sleep. I suppose it was her way of trying to replace Mamma in my life. With me being eight or nine years old, my feet dragged on the floor as she rocked, but I loved it. She was doing a good job of trying to comfort the youngest child, who was left without parents. She loved us and worried about us; always made a big fuss if we were not clean about ourselves and the house; saw to it that we went to Church; and when the young boys started to come sniffing around after Mae and Theta as soon as they were of age, she did not let them hang around too late in the night but would send them packing early in the evening.

"We don't want people to have anything to talk about." The gossip was that all us girls would get in trouble and have babies out of wedlock.

We kept the house nice and clean, Mae, Theta, and I, with me running behind trying to help. Right after our breakfast, Mae, Theta and I would go upstairs and make beds in all three bedrooms, leaving the rooms nice and clean; carry down the coal oil lamps and slop buckets; empty the slop buckets, wash them and put in a cleaning solution of Lysol in water, leaving them out in the field until evening; clean the outhouse from time to time; refill the lamps; wash the lamp chimneys; clean and polish the stove with blackening; set the yeast for baking bread (this was to mix a paste of yeast, salt and water), and allow it to set over night; wash the clothes in a wooden washtub, scrub them on a wooden scrub board with a galvanized steel scrubbing surface; hang the clothes on the line, throwing some on the low bushes for the sun to bleach; scrub the wooden floors; go to the fields and pastures to gather apples and berries.

Mae and Theta were very close in age and, like sisters, they did not always get along and had some tough arguments that sometimes came to blows — scratching and pulling hair — but this did not last long. Mostly we sang when we worked, usually hymns that Mamma had taught us. Mae has a beautiful soprano voice, Theta a lower soprano, and I sang alto. I did not know I was singing alto but they would always exclaim, "Christie is singing alto." They would test me by singing something that had very hard alto notes, then scream laughing when I would make the note. "She made it, she hit that note!" We had such fun singing. Later in life we were told that people would stop and listen as they passed our house, and talked of how well we sang, but we were not aware of this at the time. We just sang because we loved to.

I loved to play with dolls and mud cakes out under the apple tree with Theta, who was, to my way of thinking, really another me. Theta and I shared many things

— secrets, toys, food, cuddling close together in the night when a thunderstorm came up; Theta pulling me by the hand when we were late going to school; telling me to walk behind her when there was a big snow storm when we were coming home from school or from Weymouth town, using her body to ward off the cold wind. I can see her now with her chestnut brown skin and big black eyes that would give a very angry stare at anyone who would start to harm Frankie or me. I have seen her fly in the face of the tough boys at school who would start to pick on us. I felt so safe when Theta was going to school with us. But when Mae left home to go to work in Halifax, Theta stayed at home to be the housekeeper. Now there were three of us at home, Theta, Frankie and me, with Lottie coming home each night.

I cannot recall exactly when, or why, Mae left to go to work in Halifax, but soon she was gone. I thought she was doing a good job keeping house and looking after us with the help of Theta. She was very strict. With her as boss, we had to toe the line or she would give us a cuff up side the head, but Mae was very passionate and caring. If one of us were sick, Mae would make what she called "the sick chair." Putting two chairs together in the corner by the stove and using quilts, pillows and coats, she made a comfortable bed. And there she made you stay until she thought you were well enough. And always she would be bringing some awful tasting stuff for us to take. Mae loved to be boss. I think that is why she and Theta could not get along. With being so close in age it was hard for one to take orders from the other, so they often came to blows. But they never fought with me: they fought around, or over, but never with me, both being very good to me. When we were all in the bed, which we had to share, with me in the middle, they fought, hitting at each other across my head but never touching me. They would each pull so hard on the quilt, with both pulling in the opposite direction, I was quite safe and warm, but the quilt never touched me all night. It was pulled so

The War Years

The news of a war breaking out meant nothing to me. World affairs were the farthest thing from my mind until on one of those pleasant Sundays when all the family was at home, and along with the preparing of dinner, I heard mention of Europe, England, Germany. But what caused me to sit up and take notice was hearing Harold say, "I am joining the army." Some members of the family were trying to discourage him from going but Harold was convincing them that it would be good for the family because he would be able to send money home to help. So, Harold joined the army and it was not long before we started losing all our brothers, as Bernard was next, then Irving and Guy were preparing to go. One had to be eighteen years old to join up. Guy lied about his age and, along with a cousin, Sydney Cromwell, and Irving, Guy was gone.

So now four of our loving brothers were gone, enlisted in the army: to train in army camps all over Canada; to be taught how to fight to kill; and to eventually go overseas and join in the war in Europe. Weymouth Falls had many young men who willingly joined the army to protect their country; to travel over some of the world; and to be able to make money to send home to their families. However, at the beginning of the war, Black men had been refused when they offered to join. They were told, "No this is a white man's war!" But as things got worse, the war in Europe became real bad, and they began to run out of men to send. Now they were only too happy to accept Black men, who were very proud to help protect their country. Weymouth Falls alone had more than fifty men, young and old, from seventeen to forty-five, who joined up.

Even our small town was involved in the war effort. Everything from paper to iron, rubber, stone, tin — many such things were sent to the war factories to be turned into bombs or whatever was needed for the war. So we went around gathering everything we could find, then piled it all by our gate for the army trucks to pick up. This made us feel like we were helping our brothers win the war. Everett remained at home so we were content to know we had our quiet easy-going brother at home, though it was both frightening and sad to see the other four go overseas, not knowing if they would return. Lottie had asked Everett to stay with us. After all, we needed at least one of our big brothers to stay at home with us. This did not last long, for the Troop Train, which came through all the towns at this time looking for young men who were willing to join the army, came to Weymouth.

Everett was downtown at the time with Lottie. Lots of young men were going to the train to join up — white and Black men — men Everett had gone to school with, or worked with. Lottie said Everett looked so sad as he watched them all go. Lottie could no longer deny him the chance to go, so she said, "Go on Everett." Well, she hardly got the words out of her mouth when he was gone, darting back to hug and thank her, he was off like the others.

The day Everett left to go off to one of the training camps will always remain etched in my memory. Frankie, who took it the hardest, was out in his little shack he had built for himself. No one was allowed into his little wooden shack, not even me. Frankie went into his shack whenever he was upset, lonely or angry; today he was in his shack because he did not want Everett to go. Theta was playing a sad tune on the guitar; I was sitting on the front doorstep watching him go, walking proudly down the road in his new suit. We had all screamed with joy the day he came home with a new suit, shoes and felt hat. We were so happy he had finally gotten something for himself. He had always spent the meagre wages he got on the family. Now that he had grown to a tall handsome man and all the girls were chasing him, he needed to look good when going to church functions and all. Now he was wearing his nice new things to go to war. We did not openly cry when he said good-bye to us, though tears were just in the back of our eyes. I went looking for Frankie after Everett had gone, and taking a chance, I peeked into his little shack, finding him all humped up in the corner crying. "I wanted Everett to stay at home to help me with the chores," Frankie said.

So all five of our big brothers were gone. They were allowed to come home on leave now and then, after months of rigorous training. Each of them, in turn, had come home on weekend visits and had brought with them young men from some of the other coloured villages in Canada. Everett got only one leave to come home. We were all jumping and shouting with joy when he came in the gate, this tall handsome soldier, with lots of packs on his back and a guitar, which he gave to me. As we all sat around him, listening to his every word, we noticed that he wore a rope-like string around his neck. When we asked him what it was, he took it out of the neck of his shirt, and hanging on the rope chain was a round thing with numbers on it, which he said was his "dog tags" with his platoon number on it. Then he explained that he was on embarkation leave and he would be able to stay home for thirty days before going overseas. Though we were happy to have him home, it was a letdown knowing he would go to England when he left.

It was not the same with Mae gone, with just Theta, Frankie and me at home during the day and Lottie coming home in the evening. The home became very lonely and sad, when there had always been so many people and so much fun and laughter. One winter, when we had a very heavy snowstorm, (these snowstorms can come up with no warning in Nova Scotia), we had had a hard time getting home from school through the storm that day, and now Lottie was not home from work and it was getting late. We were getting very worried. Uncle Roy came down the hill to check up on us. He was always watching from his house up on the hill, I suppose to see if we were all right. Now he could see that Lottie had not arrived home. And so we waited. Uncle Roy paced up and down the floor, looking from window to window, saying to himself, "Ah sugar... Ah shoot... what a storm... Ah shaw, she'll soon be home, don't worry... Ah sugar." These were his swear words, he would never say a bad word. Theta, Frankie and I sat by the stove getting more and more worried by the minute. Finally we heard some people talking, and rushing to the window we could see Lottie with some of the other women coming up the road, which was packed with snow, the women up to their knees in snow. When Lottie finally came into the house, we rushed to help her out of her things and helped to make her warm by the stove. But as she sat near the stove her face began to swell and she could not stop shaking. Her face grew bigger and bigger. We were so frightened we did not know what to do, and she was beginning to look real awful. Uncle Roy disappeared, then came back very quickly with Aunt Girlie right behind. "Lottie you lay down," Aunt Girlie demanded, and she covered her up nice and tight. She had brought with her some fish skin and vinegar, and she put the skin on the stove to heat. She then put the hot fish skin in the vinegar and the fish skin around Lottie's throat. She poured some more vinegar on the fish skin, wrapped Lottie all up warm, and in no time, Lottie's face was back to normal again. Thank God for Aunt Girlie and Uncle Roy!

Lottie had made the house very cozy and the kitchen so warm and comfortable in winter by adding a new pantry, rearranging the table so it was closer to the stove, and repairing the doors and windows. Lottie worked hard to keep us warm, fed and happy. She would even put on her brother's old clothes and help to carry wood from the woods.

Once when Frankie was sick with a cold or something, he had refused to eat the delicious stew and hot biscuits Lottie had made. This was a shock as Frankie would never turn down food. "Won't you even have a hot biscuit?" Lottie asked. "Well perhaps a half of one," Frankie said, and accepted it, eating it slowly. Not long after, he said, "Ah, Lottie, can I have another half of a biscuit please," then soon after, "Please can I have another half of a biscuit?"

Theta said, "My goodness, Frankie is eating more than we are, eating biscuits by the half." Now when all the family are together and biscuits are being served, one of us will always say, "Oh, I will just have a half of a biscuit," which will always start us laughing and teasing Frankie.

The war in Europe went on and on. We had a small battery radio and would gather around to listen to the news each night, which was always full of terrible reports. All the talk everywhere was always of the war. The newspapers contained pictures of men lost or wounded in action. We would stare at these pictures with great sadness, for we did not want anyone to be as hurt as we would be if it were one of our brothers. It seemed it would never end, this awful war, and would our young men ever come back? And if they did, would they be the same?

We wrote many letters to them and we sometimes received letters from them. How we would gather close to Lottie as she read letters from our brothers, though they could not tell much of what was taking place there because it was forbidden to write anything about the situation. Lottie, and all of the families who had boys oversees, each month sent boxes of much-needed goods to the boys. Lottie had to pack six boxes that she sent to her friend Jimmie. These boxes were wrapped in very strong paper, then wrapped in cloth and sown tightly with twine for safety. Years later we heard that the boys had not received all these packages, just one or two.

We wondered always... will we ever see our brothers again? Will they come home after this is over? Perhaps with the life they are leading there, seeing all of Europe, they may not wish to come back to these small towns. With this thought in mind, some of the young girls who were waiting for their boyfriends to return just gave up and married others. After all, they said, these men have been there for years, they see all sorts of pretty women; girls who we hear are very nice and friendly to our men. Why should they come back to us? So why are we waiting for them?

So hope of the war ending soon was fast fading away, it had gone on for over three years now, with no end in sight.

Meanwhile lots of changes had taken place in our home, thanks to the money that our brothers sent to us. We never again were hungry, had lots to eat, had nice clothes to wear to school, and our house took on a whole new look. We had new furniture, pretty wallpaper and curtains, a rug for the family room, a new stove for the kitchen and one in the family room, where we could sit comfortably and did not have to crowd around the kitchen stove, and mattresses for the beds instead of straw ticks. I was so proud of our house and now just loved to clean it up.

Frankie started a bad habit though — he started stealing things like sugar, anything he could get his hands on that was sweet. He would even steal the candy bars that Lottie was saving to send oversees to the boys. Lottie scolded Frankie over and over about stealing, telling him if he did not behave, he would be sent to reform school, the place were they put boys when they were bad. We had heard of reform school and how awful a place it was, so whenever I caught Frankie stealing I would try to stop him, saying, "Frankie, stop, or you will have to go to form school" (I did not know how to pronounce it). Once he said, "Well, Lottie sends all the good stuff to my brothers, and none for me." I felt awful when he said that, and it made me realize just how hard it was for Frankie to lose all of his big brothers, how unfair it all was. We were doing great with lots to eat and plenty of clothing to wear, but we had been so happy when we were hungry and all ten of us were at home.

One Saturday when Lottie was up at the church, busy with some church work, and Theta, Frankie and I were at home, we saw two tall White men coming in the gate. We were so frightened, we did not know what to do. They had on uniforms with two big letters on their arm — M.P. They did not knock but came right into the house. Frankie scooted out as they came in, and Theta and I stood there shaking. I remember Theta answering all of their questions as politely as she could, with her head up, looking them straight in the face with her saucy look, letting them know she was the boss and pretending not to be afraid. After she told them where Lottie was, they left and went up the road. Soon they brought Lottie home and she went upstairs, with them right behind her, with Theta and I following. Lottie looked on her dresser among lots of letters and got out one of the letters we had gotten from Irving, who was overseas. After looking at the letter, they left, and Lottie explained that Irving had received his notice from the Armed Forces to report for duty. Since he was already in the army Lottie did not think it necessary to reply. So they thought he was ducking the army, but he was already serving his country.

Well, we finally calmed down enough to wonder where Frankie was. We found him out in his shack, all curled up in a corner, bawling his eyes out. "The police came to take me to form school," he said. "No, Frankie," we exclaimed, "they don't want you, they wanted Irving" I can still see the look of relief on his face, and when we started to explain it all to him, Frankie's big hazel eyes brightened up. It goes without saying Frankie never stole ever again.

Theta and I were certainly not without fault. Lottie ran a small credit monthly at one store in town and we were often sent to the town to buy small items. We would credit candy or cookies and eat them before we arrived home, so we were stealing also, not from Lottie, but from our brothers, who were sending us monies to help support us.

Because there were not many men to work in the factories and at other labour jobs, women were accepted as workers at factories ad war plants that sprang up all over Canada. Many of the young women from our town, and others, left home to seek out work in these plants or factories. It was a known fact that in normal times, regardless of how much education a coloured girl had, she could only find employment as a teacher or nurse, or the more menial jobs like housemaid. So the jobs at the factories sounded good, because the wages were attractive.

Theta decided to go to Bridgetown to work in the apple factory. This sounded so good to Lottie that she also decided to go. Now, what to do with Frankie and me? We did not have to wonder where Frankie would go for he already spent most of his time at Aunt Gert's and she was more than happy to have Frankie stay with her. But when I asked if I could stay, she laughed her loud laugh and said, "No child, I don't want no girl-child on my hands, girls are too much trouble," and she threw her head back with her big laugh, "Jesus Lord no, child, ha-ha-ha." That was Aunt Gert, saying exactly what she meant, though she welcomed me when I went up with Frankie. We loved to sit on her cozy covered lounge and listen to her tell of her life when she was young. Always laughing, mostly at herself, she found it so funny when she forgot something as older folk do and we would laugh right along with her.

One day she put a large piece of butter in the stove instead of in the frying pan and then wondered were the butter went. She laughed so when we told her what she had done. We spent many days listening to her tell stories and eating her delicious tea biscuits. We caught her smoking a corncob pipe once. As we walked in one day, there she sat, smoking her pipe. When she saw us, she threw it in the woodbox behind the stove. We pretended not to notice and had many good laughs about it after. Her brother lived right up the hill and that would be a perfect place for me to stay.

Uncle George and Aunt Hattie had seven grown children, most of whom were married and living away. Two of their sons, George and Vernon, had also joined the army and were overseas. The home of Uncle George and Aunt Hattie was always full of life and it would be as if I was right with Frankie, for Aunt Gert spent most of her evenings up at her brother's, and there Frankie and I would be, together. However, this was not to be. It was decided that I would stay with Uncle Roy and Aunt Girlie.

Now I liked them all right, but I just did not feel at home with them — they were not full of fun like Uncle George. But in those days, one never questioned one's elders, and Lottie had had a long talk with Aunt Girlie and they decided where I would stay, and that was that. I was thirteen, would be fourteen this coming Christmas, a tall, skinny, funny-looking, gangly-legged girl. I was getting on better at school now, coming out of my shell. I found it easier to make friends; still hated boys though, could not stand them to touch me. Although I was treated very nicely at the home of my aunt and uncle, I was very lonely. From up on this hill I could look down at our house. It was so gray and bare with the windows all boarded up, so quiet and empty.

Lottie and Theta had gotten jobs at the factory in Bridgetown, but Lottie had suffered an injury and was rushed to the nearby hospital in Middleton. This injury was of the hip area and she would have to remain in hospital to convalesce for some time. We knew not for how long. Beulah, Aunt Girlie's daughter, and Theta, took me to visit Lottie at the hospital. She looked so pretty there, covered with white sheets, and was so happy to see us.

As Christmas drew near, Theta told me in one of her many letters that she would go to the hospital and spend Christmas with Lottie, and I thought that was a good idea. Hospital would be a very lonely place to spend Christmas. All preparations were being made for the holidays at my aunt and uncle's home — their family was all at home: Beulah,

Joyce and all the grandchildren. They were rejoicing and having a wonderful time.

It was Christmas Eve, with the sounds of horse-drawn sleighs and ox-teams going past, families going home from shopping, their teams all trimmed with bells and ribbons, the bells ringing, people shouting "Merry Christmas" as they went by. I had asked if I could go up the road to spend Christmas Eve with Frankie but received a flat "No" from Aunt Girlie, "I know Gert will go up to George's and they will all be drinking and the Lord knows what will go on up there. I am responsible for you while you are here and I don't want anything to happen to you with your sister in the hospital and all." This was not very surprising for I had not been allowed to go up the road to stay after dark, and when I visited Frankie at Aunt Gert's, I had to leave and be home before it got too dark. But I had hoped she would understand I wanted to be with my brother on this night before Christmas. And she was correct; we would all end up at Uncle George's and having a ball. Uncle George and his guests would all get a little tipsy from their home brew, and there would be dancing and lots of fun, but I knew better than to question authority. What Aunt Girlie said was the law, so to defy her never entered my mind. Trying not to let the family know how upset I was, I asked to be excused, pretending not to feel well and went up to my room.

I was lying on my bed crying, for I was so lonely and I knew Frankie was having a great time by now up at Uncle George's. I thought I heard someone call my name from the road. Running down the stairs I exclaimed, "Someone is calling me from the road."

"No, no one is calling. How can you hear if someone is calling you with all that noise those people are making going by?" Aunt Girlie said with her quick sharp voice, "You said you did not feel well. Then go up and rest. You will feel better in the morning. You must be better for Christmas," and with a pleasant little pat she dismissed me.

Back up in my room I lay on the bed and soon again heard my name called. This time I did not hesitate but ran down the stairs, and grabbing my coat and boots, I was out the door, running down through the falling snow, down the long gap that led to the road. Now I could see through the heavy snow who it was. Theta, with a beautiful new winter outfit, hat and coat, her pretty sharp eyes sparkling through the snow, laughed loudly at my excitement in seeing her. "Did you think we would let you spend Christmas and your birthday alone?" she asked as she grabbed me and we hugged each other hard, not even noticing the cold or the snow, after jumping up and down with many hugs and kisses. And now I saw all the luggage she had. The taxi had dropped her off and she was calling me to help her in with all the luggage and packages. She had brought many gifts for both Frankie and me. "When I told you I was spending Christmas with Lottie we had it all planned," explained Theta. "I visited her at the hospital and she and I ordered all these gifts from the catalogue. It was such fun. Lottie said it made her feel as if she was at home and preparing for Christmas." So Theta, Frankie and I spent a wonderful Christmas together.

Another wonderful thing happened that winter. Our brother Harold was sent home. Calling it wonderful seems out of place, for he was sent home because he had tuberculosis. He had been in hospital in England and was very unhappy when they said he was to come home because he wanted to stay over in Europe as his brothers were still there. He told us that Everett, when learning that he was in hospital, came to visit him. As wonderful as it was to have him visit, Harold said he cried like a baby when he heard the sound of Everett's boots walking away down the corridor.

It was frightening when we learned that Harold was on the hospital ship coming home for we did not know what condition he was in. There was so much secrecy about the movements of the soldiers that we never knew if the men were wounded in action or sick until the newspaper or the radio announced it. There was always just a list of ships, of men who were coming home, their rank, number and name, so it was somewhat of a relief when we learned that Harold was not in real bad condition but had contracted T.B. and "no wonder" with the conditions they had to endure, lying in trenches in the wet and all kinds of weather. It certainly was terrible for those young boys who had to very quickly become men.

Harold was admitted into the Camp Hill Hospital in Halifax and convalesced there for some months, and now he was well enough to come home. I got a big surprise one evening when I answered a knock on the door and there stood Harold. How shy I was when I first saw him, this heavy-set handsome man with a thick black mustache and long sideburns, looking so serious and not at all like the happy-go-lucky young boy who would come riding up on his bike with a funny story to make us laugh. I just stood with my head down, too shy to say more than, "Hi Harold."

In no time, with the help of Frankie, Harold repaired and fixed, painted and cleaned, until the old house looked like new. Soon Lottie was well enough to come home. How happy this girl was when Theta and Lottie arrived home and we were all home again, all that is except Bernard, Irving, Everett, Guy and Mae, but it was not long before the war came to an end. At the announcement of the war's end, all the people marched up and down the road shouting, singing and banging on pots, pans, tubs, washboards and anything that made a noise. The war was over at last! Our boys were coming home! The thing to do now was to watch the newspaper for the announcements of troop ships returning, and who was on each ship, and if they were coming home, for it was said that some of the men had married women there and would remain in Europe. We also wondered what condition they would be in after these terrible experiences.

Bernard was the first to arrive home. Taller than I

remembered, still as serious as ever, he did not stay around long but was, in no time, working in the woods again. He always said he was a woodsman. We got all excited when we read Corpl. I. D. Cromwell in the lists of soldiers arriving on the next ship. We all met him at the station. Smiling, cute, dancing eyebrows, short stocky Irving. Loaded down with packs on his back, his smile was the same but he had a strained look behind that smile. He had gone through hell over there. A hell we could never ever imagine. Irving's platoon was a gunner troop, which handles one of the large guns. It took about five or six men to handle this gun. Irving's job was to help feed the shells into the gun. The noise of the gun; waiting many days down in trenches; watching men get blown up and die just steps away; having friends die right in the trench beside you; and always thinking the next shell had your name on it.

Irving could not and would not tell us of all this but tried to cover it up and enjoy being at home at last, though he seemed very restless and wanted to go places all the time. After all the travel and having to rush and "jump to it" on command, it was so hard to adjust to this slow pace here in this small town. Now that was all over but it would not ever be over for Irving or any of those young men who went through it. Though he was not able to talk about it at the time, he would tell us of his getting in and out of trouble; of all the countries he had seen; and the people, how welcoming the people of England, Holland, Belgium, France, Germany and all of Europe were to them. It was not long before he was sitting by the stove, telling us fantastic stories.

Mount Beulah United Baptist Church, Weymouth Falls, was established in 1853 on this the original site.

St. Matthew's Anglican Church in Weymouth Falls was established in 1900 and is the only Black Anglican church in North America

After the War

Our house was taking on the same look and feel it had before the war. Mae was married by now and living in Dartmouth; she had married Victor Samuels, of Dartmouth. Theta had come home with Lottie and stayed for a long visit, helping to get the house in order. She too was to be married, to a James Jackson of Inglewood, Bridgetown.

Now that I was fourteen years old, I could see many things in a different light. For instance, I had never noticed just how pretty Lottie was and now that she was expecting her boyfriend Jimmie to come home, she was simply glowing. From the time I could remember, there was always Lottie and Jimmie, Jimmie and Lottie. We all knew they would marry some day. Like all the young men, Jimmie had joined up as soon as the war started. Now he was coming home. Jimmie Dearing was his parents' only son. Lottie was like a young teenager now, having her Jimmy home again, and soon there would be plans for their wedding. However, when Jimmy went for his final discharge, it was discovered he had tuberculosis and would have to go to the sanatorium, remaining there for treatment for we knew not how long, This was a very hard blow for Lottie and all of us. She had waited through the war for him and now she must continue to wait.

So now there were seven of us home, though Theta had to go back to Bridgetown to work and prepare for her marriage. By now all the men had found jobs — Bernard in the forest, Irving at a garage in Digby — but they would all be coming home for Christmas.

It was Christmas Eve, Lottie is trimming the tree; just she and I are there. I am so comfortable... proud and happy with our place. The house is so nicely cleaned up, with all the new furniture. I was so proud of our home. Helping to trim the tree and talking with Lottie, the afternoon was perfect. We had seen Guy's name in the list of returning service men. He would be home for New Year's.

I am all dressed up in the latest fashion, dirndl skirt, bobby socks and penny loafers, my hair brushed back in a ponytail as I waited for the arrival of our brothers; I just knew they would be home for Christmas. It was growing late and I was starting to get worried. The only train that came through Weymouth had passed and there had been enough time for them to come home. Joyce, Aunt Girlie's daughter who lived in Bridgetown, had arrived that day on the train — it was nice to see cousin Joyce — the first words out of my mouth were, "Hi Joyce, did you see our brothers on the train?" "Hi Christie, no," she said in her mother's quick voice, and turning to Lottie they went into lots of talk about Bridgetown and their friends there. I waited until there was a time I could cut in and asked again. "Joyce, did you come down on the train?" With a quick look at me she said "Yes," then back to Lottie, and continued their conversation.

"Well did you see any of our brothers on the train?" I interrupt very rudely. Again I get a quick "no," with Joyce not even bothering to look at me. I stop trimming the tree and sit down by the stove, very sad. By now I should be accustomed to being disappointed; I had been let down so often in the past, but I had so hoped they would be home for Christmas. The cheers and shouts of Merry Christmas are coming from the road as always, though cars had replaced most of the horse-drawn sleds and ox teams. Now I also hear singing, men's voices, and they sound familiar. We

Cromwell veterans: l to r: Irving, Everett, and Guy

Everett Cromwell

Above: Lottie, Christie and Theta. Right: Christie at a party in the 1950s

Right: Albert in the 1950s, Christie in her twenties

knew it was our brothers and lots of men, returned soldiers, walking up the road, with arms around each other, singing at the top of their voices, "Sweet Adeline." Joyce and Lottie were both grinning at me now. They were trying to keep a secret, wanting to surprise me. Well, this was a lovely surprise. It turned out to be a lovely Christmas!

Guy arrived home on New Year's Eve. All the family but me went to meet him at the train. This was a great reunion; many family and friends were there to meet him and the many other men who came home on that day. He and most of the men now arriving had all seen some heavy war battles. Guy had been in the ground troops, and having to fight in hand-to-hand combat, left him shell-shocked. He was shot in the buttocks and came close to being shot many other times. He also saw his comrades shot down right before his eyes. Guy told us later, much later, of a time when he was face-to-face with a very young German soldier, who looked to be about seventeen. He was crouched down in a corner of a bombed-out building; his blonde hair and big blue eyes were shining in the sun; he was shaking with fright for he knew he was to be killed. They both continued to stare at each other and Guy could not shoot. He allowed the young man to creep away. Thank the good Lord he was now at home.

Why was I not at the station to meet Guy? Lottie asked me to stay at home with Gramma, who lived in Boston, who sent us second-hand clothes in a barrel now and then. This was the woman to whom our mother often wrote and to whom she had writen on her deathbed we don't know what; perhaps she asked her to come home, as she did not think she would live. Perhaps she pleaded, "Please come and be here with my children in their time of need. Act like a grandmother."

Frankie and I often talked about the fact that we knew we had a grandmother and we even expected that she — or one of our relatives — would come home. Mamma had two half-sisters and other relatives there in Boston, and because we imagined them to be rich, we talked of them bringing us gifts and money. So that summer when all was wonderful and the war had ended and we needed nothing from our relatives in Boston, Lottie said, "Your grandmother is coming home." Well, she came alright, stepping gingerly out of a taxi, looking like a very rich white woman, or I should say, looking very white and all glittering with gold jewellery. I have to admit she was quite pretty, but I had already made up my mind not to like her. I knew if I asked, "Why didn't you come home when your daughter needed you?" I would have been in big trouble so I kept my mouth shut and tried to treat her like a grandmother. But to make matters worse she bragged about her grandchildren in Boston, how well they did in school. I wanted to say, "It is no wonder they do so good with all the help they get from you," but I told myself to shut up.

Lottie seemed so happy to have her and bestowed all the attention on her, taking her here and there, visiting all the people of Weymouth Falls and in the town. Bernard, Irving and Harold couldn't do enough for her and gave her lots of the souvenirs they had brought from Europe. They said she looked just like mamma. Well, the treatment they were giving her should have been given to Lottie, who they left to look after us and all the responsibility of the home. I could not see any resemblance of my mother in her, with her pale face; she was a sister to our beloved aunts here, Hattie and Girlie, and to Uncle Rod. But she did not have the pretty brown biscuit complexion or smile like them. She must have lots of make up on, I thought, but I kept my mouth shut.

Now back to New Year's and Guy's arriving. He also was shocked when arriving in the house and seeing Gramma. Welcoming her with open arms, he said "I thought for a minute you were Mamma sitting there." As he hugged her, everyone was talking and laughing at the same time. "I saved you Christmas," Lottie said as she came from the pantry with all the delicious foods we had enjoyed at

Christmas. Whilst all this was going on I stood quietly in the corner behind the stove, staring at this big tall handsome soldier who was pretending to be Guy. This was not the Guy I remembered at all, the skinny brat who came whistling or singing down the road from Aunt Gert's, who would hit and tease us. Who took me for rides on the sledge in winter and, when my hands ached from the cold, would hold them and give a big slap to them and make them stop aching. No, this was not Guy.

Then the stranger spotted me standing there. "Who is this?" he asked. "That is Christie, Guy," Lottie said in a surprised voice, wondering why he did not know me. He just stared at me for a time, then shouted, "Lena Horne!" and grabbed me up in his big arms. "Jeepers, creepers... Holy smut, Christie, you are a pretty young lady now," he was saying as he was swinging me up in the air, laughing and sounding just like Guy. He held onto me the rest of the evening. At one time Lottie said, "Christie, it is past your bedtime," but Guy said, "Oh, let her stay up. We all have to be together to celebrate being home for Christmas." We all sat and talked nearly all night, remembering all the good and bad things, and again laughing, as our family must.

Now the last brother remaining in Europe was Everett. The one we did not want to see go was still not at home. He had volunteered to stay over there to help with the clean-up after the war. Our young men had not all come back unharmed, if not physically, then medically. Guy had been shell-shocked; Irving had bad nerves; Harold contracted tuberculosis. Our cousin Vernon, Uncle George's son, got shot in the leg and was crippled for life. He said he had to drag himself for hours with his leg hanging on by a small bit of skin until he was found. There are many others I do not know about. Quinton Sparks was killed in action. But as I said before, the news that struck our home very hard was about Jimmie Dearing having to remain in the sanatorium for an indefinite period of time. He and Lottie had planned to get married as soon as he came home but now they would have to wait longer.

When the year was up Everett finally came home. We were all there to meet him; another tall, handsome soldier stepped down from the train. As we walked through the Town of Weymouth, many of the townsfolk came rushing to greet him and shake his hand. Some merchants came out of their stores to welcome him. The town seemed to have a great respect for and pride in all the young men who went to war to defend their country. As a show of appreciation, all veterans were given a sum of money. This was a gratuity from the government, and this gave them a start to try to rebuild their lives again. Many built homes, or did what ever they wished.

Now the people all over gave parties, dances, dinners and many functions to show the veterans that we all appreciated them and wanted to show them a good time. However, the church leaders of Weymouth Falls would not allow dancing in their church halls. Though they gave dinners and concerts and so on to welcome them home, at the end of the festivities they would announce there would be no dancing, though the people expected it, so the young people had to go elsewhere to dance. We all found this very unfair, so Harold came up with an idea to build a dancehall. And so, just up the road from our house — across from Uncle Roy's — Harold began to build his dancehall. He got lots of protests from the people on the Falls Road, but he went on with his plan and in the evenings we could hear him hammering and pounding away.

Soon it was not just him alone, for other young men came to help. While some of the older men sort of stood around watching, I was always there as soon as I came home from school and my chores were finished. Up to the hall I would run. Harold allowed me to do little chores for him, which I was only too happy to do. I wanted the hall to be finished as soon as possible for I loved to dance. I was still a little shy when it came to talk but dancing was different. We did not have to like the boy or talk to the boy just go to the party or dancehall, and if asked we just danced with all who would ask — not like today. Now if a boy asks you to dance you look to see if he is cute or has on the right clothes or whatever. We just danced with whoever. It would be an insult to refuse the boys and they would never ask anyone again.

So we danced the jitterbug, boogie-woogie, all the popular dances. We had a real ball and no one said you had to dance with only one partner all evening. It was just a ball! When the hall was complete, Harold hung a sign on the front:

Vets Hangout, Sat. Night,
Dancing from Eight to Twelve

At eight o'clock sharp on that Saturday night the music started. You could hear it all over Weymouth Falls Road. I can still remember his first theme song. "I'm tipping in, tip-tipping in, I'd better take my shoes off, I'm tipping in." When we heard this music, young boys and girls came from everywhere, all decked out in our dancing clothes. The price was thirty-five cents. Harold had all the latest records, and in our dirndl skirts, bobby socks and saddle oxfords, with snapping fingers, we jitter-bugged like crazy to the hot boogie-woogie sounds. When the time came to close, no one wanted to leave. Each week Harold had a hard time closing the place. Everyone wanted to dance on, so he put up a new sign:

Dancing from Eight to---?

The hall was not just for dancing, but for all veterans. Young men could hang out there during the week and play cards or pool — it was a sort of release for young men or old to just be men and get away — though Harold did not allow alcohol at the dances. Some of the people of the Falls Road objected very much to the Vets Hangout, and vowed their children would never go to that awful place, but some of the children would sneak there anyway. We heard stories of some climbing out of their windows when their parents thought they were in bed, and shimmying down a tree, then running to the Vets Hangout.

We would all get a big laugh when they would come walking in so cool as if they were free to come. Not one of us would tell on them. No other teenage girl could be as happy as this one in those days. I was the only girl at home during the day, though still in school, so I kept house. All the brothers were back doing the same sort of work they did before the war, though Everett worked at the sawmill now, and Harold and Guy worked and lived in Halifax. Those men, who had been all over Europe, were now back doing the same jobs and being treated as if they had not just fought in a great war, where their lives could have been ended any second. How soon they forget.

So I was having the most wonderful life. Everett was not home long before he bought me a lovely new coat, and for Christmas I received many new clothes from my family. Everett said he wanted me to stay in school; he would pay for my education. So I was dressed as well as all the other girls in school, had lots of friends and started to like school, the higher grades being much more interesting.

I would be fifteen on my birthday the coming Christmas and what a summer we had! Mae came with her husband and baby girl, Cheryl, and Theta with her new husband and baby boy, Everett. All ten of us stood in the kitchen and drank a toast with wine. Even Frankie and I were allowed a glass of wine.

Mae, Theta and I just had to get into our silly dancing. There we were, on the porch, one striking out a tune and the other striking a step, just like old times, when a caterpillar dropped down from the ceiling. Well, you talk about trying to all get out of there at the same time, screaming and grabbing at each other. All three of us are very afraid of caterpillars — to even write the word makes my skin crawl.

And so life was perfect and suddenly I liked boys — and

there were lots of boys to choose from whenever there was a function in Weymouth Falls. The Harvest Suppers (there were two in Weymouth Falls, one put on by the Anglican Church, the other by the Baptist Church), were the most important functions in all of the Black communities. Everyone attended, tickets were sold and people came from all the communities to each one. Even white people bought tickets and came to the suppers, though they came and left early. I did not know why they did not stick around for the real fun after. But the suppers were delicious, with homemade foods made from the harvest — chicken, ham, vegetables, pies, cakes and homemade ice cream. After the suppers were all sold and there was food left over, there would be an auction. What fun it would be to listen to the men bidding higher and higher for a cake or pie, and then the tables would be put back out of the way, and the room would be made ready for square-dancing. That was before the war though, and now that dancing was not allowed, we all went down to the Vets Hangout and danced the night away. Each weekend there was something going on, if not in Weymouth, then in another village.

Now remember old big-head Albert? Well, by now he had grown to be a heavy-set seventeen-year-old working at the sawmill. He thought he was a big man now, still coming around, still teasing me, hanging around with my brothers. I didn't hate him as I used to — in fact, I sort of liked him.

Our home was always full of young people, mostly on the weekend. There was always music playing, dancing or card games. I received no attention from most of the young men, though there were some I had eyes for, but Albert was the only one who paid any attention to me, this skinny girl. I had long black hair, which I wore in a page boy style, curled under and sitting on my shoulders. I had big sad eyes and always looked down when approached by anyone, still shy. So it was nice when a boy would come to me for a dance for I did not have to talk, just dance, grab a hand, get on the floor and swirl and twirl, jitter-bug, snapping fingers and go, go, go!

Albert became a dispatcher at Taylor's Mill, working with the driver, and was allowed to bring the truck home some weekends. Now he could drive us kids to the movies and all. We would all jump on the truck, and off we went, wherever we wished. Albert started having me get in the front with him; this was to show the others that I was his girl. Once, when we were driving home from a movie, he asked me for a kiss. I said, "No, not here, everyone would see us." "Well look," he said, "all the others are doing it, and when I looked everyone on the truck was in an embrace, hugging and kissing." I turned my face to Albert and we kissed.

This was my first kiss and it was wonderful. The moon and stars looked brighter; the night was warmer; there was singing in the air, so whenever we could, without wrecking the truck, we kissed. So now old big-head Albert was my beau (as we called it then), and so through the cold of winter or the hot summer we went everywhere together — all young people having lots of fun together.

Though our brothers were not in the same places when in the army overseas, they sometimes got the opportunity to see each other. They told us of how nice it was when there would be a Cromwell in the nearby troop and they could go and visit each other, to be able to bring each other up to date as to what was happening at home. Bernard had learned that the only brother left at home was Frankie, so he knew one of them had to try and return to help look after things there. This opportunity came when he found he was near to Irving's camp. How they loved to get together and go to an English pub for beer, or a bar in whatever country they happened to be in. So Bernard asked Irving if he could try to get home to help Lottie and look after the homestead. Irving agreed with him and started right away to get his commanding officer to arrange for him to get relief to come home.

Irving said it was futile to be asking to get out of the army with the war still going on, and when he approached his commanding officer and explained the situation, the man laughed at him and told him this request was impossible and he would have to have proof that he was really needed at home.

So Irving wrote to three of our relatives and some of the influential people in the town of Weymouth who knew of our family. Irving was called into the office not long after, and the Captain, who was surprised to learn of how much influence Irving had, told Irving all the answers arrived in his office at the same time, and yes, Irving would be able to get his discharge to go home to help his family. However, it took so long with all the paperwork that the war was over before Irving's orders came through.

Irving had decided that when he came home he would take over the payment of the mortgage on the house and look after Frankie and me. Irving got a good job at a garage in Digby and married a pretty girl from there, Eva Barton. I was her bridesmaid and for the first time wore a pretty long blue dress and felt like a Black queen. So here I am in my comfortable world, not knowing what was going on with the planning of the family. None of this had been told to me. I learned much later of Irving's trying to come home; of his plan to take over the paying for the house; I was just going happily along in my happy little world.

Now there were lots of discussions and disagreements concerning the home, which no one talked to me about (it still held that the young ones were not told of anything... not even why Mamma got sick and passed away... or why Gramma did not come when we needed her), and now there was all this unrest in the family. I did not understand it and was not informed about it.

Then came the evening when they all sat talking in the kitchen — Irving and his wife Eva were visiting with their little baby girl, Linda. Listening to the talk, I realized that Irving was coming to live permanently in the house with his family. Irving had bought the house and would be moving in. I was overjoyed. I would have Irving and Eva right here as family. Listening to what the talk had been all along I had thought this might be the case but did not really believe it, for it sounded too good to be true. I had been afraid to believe it to be true. It would be so nice to have Irving home again and Eva with little baby Linda. I had already started to plan how I would take her for walks up the road and show off that I was an aunt. Things were even better, for Guy also had married, a lovely lady from Dartmouth, Grace Samuels, and they had come to live in Aunt Gert's house, for Aunt Gert said this would be Guy's house when she was gone. So all the family seemed to be coming back home and the family was getting larger each year. I was quite in favour of all that was taking place.

This evening, Irving, Eva and I were sitting in the family room, the talk going on and on, and I overheard Lottie say that she was trying to get work near the hospital that Jimmy was in, still convalescing. Everett was considering returning to the Armed Forces. Then someone said, "What about Christie?" and I heard Bernard say, "I am not worried about Christie. I just want to be sure Frankie is looked after." My head went down low, nearly between my legs. I felt like a beaten dog. Didn't he know that Frankie and I were a package? It had always been "we have to look after the two little ones." How did we all of a sudden come apart? It was always "Frankie and Christie," so why did he not care what happened to Christie? Now I was sure Bernard did not like me. Irving, seeing how devastated I was at hearing this remark from Bernard, put his arm around me and said, "Don't worry Chris, you will always have a home here with me." Hearing this I calmed down and began to feel warm and comfortable again. Later that night Lottie told me to get my clothes and things ready, she and I would be going away to look for work.

The next day was Saturday and I saw Bernard walking up the road and ran to meet him. I was a little afraid but

I had to try. "Bernard, please can I stay at home. I want to stay in school and Everett said he would pay for my schooling. Please, I don't want to go." "No, you go with Lottie," was Bernard's reply. Without missing a step I tried to keep up with him as I kept pleading, "Please Bernard, I want to stay, Irving said I could." Bernard stopped short, turning and looking directly at me with his stern look, "Listen Christie... Irving has enough with a wife and baby and another one on the way; they don't need a teenager on their hands. No, you go with Lottie, and don't make trouble." With that, he turned and continued walking up the road.

Our search for work finally landed us in Bridgetown, where Lottie landed a good job with a nice family. Lottie's reputation had followed her and most people knew she was a good worker. I would stay with a friend of hers, Evelyn Jackson, until I found work. On the night before we left home Lottie and I were up at the Vets Hangout listening to music. I suppose we were having a sort of a good-bye to all the fun we had had there, which meant good-bye to my happy teenage years also. Though I did not know it then, our home was all closed up again with boards on the windows. There were no words spoken; we both knew we were crying.

I had been so content with all my brothers around me again. They had always spoiled me and now they had gotten into the same routine. I loved Guy's wife, Grace, and we became friends right away. Their daughter Hope was so sweet I gave her my last doll, and to me, that was a precious gift for it was the last doll Lottie had given me, and even though I had out-grown playing with dolls, I loved Marilyn. My good-bye to Albert was a little sad; we told each other we had plans to go our own separate ways. Albert was hoping to go to Ontario and perhaps get work there where his sister Gloria and brother Bob were living. I teased him, saying I had not planned to marry a boy from my hometown. "I love you Chris and always will," were

Albert's last words as he walked away with his head down, kicking at stones in the road.

My first job as a maid was with a very wealthy family. I remember visiting Lottie at her places of work. She had worked as a maid since she was thirteen, and all her employers just loved her and were very upset when she left their employment. They always spoke very well of her and wrote very glowing references of her, thus enabling her to be in great demand. Good help was always hard to get — this was not a joke. Lottie spoke of the people she worked for as if they were family, their children as if they were hers, so I expected this to be the same for me when I started working as a maid.

Though I had been brought up where I did not experience prejudice or discrimination, all white people to this young girl were different in their actions, looks, smell, walk, talk, everything... but not rude or unfriendly. Many times I had gone to meet Lottie at her work places and was always welcomed with big smiles and treats from the women she worked for, for instance Mrs. Granville, who kept a guest house. Lottie worked for her for some time. When I would go down to wait for Lottie, Mrs. Granville would just about pick me up as she wrapped her arm around me, taking me in to her large living room where there would be many men, some traveling sailors, or whatever, and say "Look at Lottie's little sister, isn't she cute?" Then she would find some of her grown daughter's old toys for me to play with and then stuff me with food.

Now, that is not to say that there were no problems between whites and blacks in Nova Scotia. It is just that I had not come up against it as yet so I was not expecting it, though I had heard and read lots about bigotry, prejudice and the fact that we, as a Black race, were thought of as a type of animal, unable to learn, unclean, on a lower level than that of the white race, and many other degrading things. Now I was facing it for the first time and I did not really know quite how to deal with it.

There were some good things about living in Bridgetown — the best one was that I got to spend lots of time with Theta, who lived just up the road in Inglewood, a lovely, clean, pretty, well-kept coloured section of Bridgetown. The Black folk of Inglewood seemed to be like one big family. I felt at home the first time I visited Inglewood when Theta got married. Now that I had come in search of work I was welcomed by all the folks of Inglewood and in no time felt like one of the families of Mitchells, Clements and Jacksons of Inglewood, and I was spending lots of time with Theta, James and their two boys, Everett (named after our brother) and Winston. Theta and I worked, shopped, took long walks and again had lots of laughs together. Her husband James was wonderful to her, seemed to worship her, and I hoped I would find a husband who treated me the same. I thought I saw this in his brother Earl, who was among the many young men and women who came to James and Theta's home most Saturday evenings to sit and talk and play cards. These evenings were wonderful and I looked forward to them.

The second nice thing was when we would all crowd into someone's car and go to the house parties or dances that would be held in all of the coloured villages. Here we got to meet other Black folk, make friends and have a great time. I was most excited when we were going to a dance in Weymouth Falls at the Vets Hangout.

Then came the time for Inglewood to have their dance, and all the folks from the other coloured villages would be coming to Inglewood. Theta and James would go, as would all of the young folk. I offered to stay with the boys but they informed me that was taken care of. Earl hardly ever attended these dances and had agreed to stay with the boys. I sort of wanted to stay at Theta's when I learned that Earl would be there, for I really had a crush on him, though he hardly even noticed me. He was about six or seven years my senior and I suppose this age difference mattered to him, but not to me. I really liked him. He had a very quiet way about him and a pleasant smile. He was always there helping his brother James with anything around his home and, like all the men in Inglewood, always helpful whenever there was something that had to be done in the village. Except for conversations between everyone at our weekend get-togethers, he and I had never had a conversation.

Many folk came from Weymouth, including Albert, who expected us to be together as a couple even though I had told him I did not wish to continue being together as boy and girl friend. Besides, my mind was on this new man I was interested in, Earl, so I faked a headache and told Theta I was going up to her place to lie down. It did not take her long to catch on. "Oh yes, you don't look too well Chris. Better go home and go right to bed. You must be coming down with something," Theta said as she winked at me, knowing what I was up to. Albert insisted on walking me up to Theta's, though it was just a little way up the road from the dancehall. As we walked, we talked of our future and I told him I was going on with my life and was not going to stay with one boy but see other people and I expected him to do the same. He was quite disappointed with me, and when he left me at Theta's gate he said before he turned to go, "Chris I still love you, but sometimes love can turn to hate." I watched him go, thinking, "This is the beginning of my new life." Though I really liked Albert, who had been very nice to me and would always be my friend, I must go on with my new life and try to forget the life I had hoped to have in Weymouth Falls.

Now what will I say when Earl answers the door — still faking a headache? I explained to him why I had come back, "You can leave now if you want, I will be here with the boys," I said as I slumped on the coach and pretended to be in pain. Earl stood over me looking very concerned, then, without a word, turned to the stove. Putting the kettle on the front of the woodstove to heat, he said, in his slow drawl, "You need a good hot cup of tea, and some rest." It was apparent he was not about to leave and it was not long before we were chatting away over a nice hot cup of tea. By the time Theta and James got home, Earl had asked me to go to the movies with him that coming Saturday. I had achieved what I had come back to do — I had gotten a date with Earl Jackson — but it does not pay when you hurt others to get what you want. Albert had been very nice to me; he did not deserve to be treated in the mean way I had treated him.

It was an exciting time being with Earl as his girl. The people in the community were surprised when they learnt that Earl was actually taking a girl out on a date in public for though he loved women and had many women who liked him, he had never openly dated a girl in Inglewood, and I shall never forget the evening we left to go to the movies. It was summer so the sun was high in the sky, even though it was evening, and all of Inglewood was, as always, out in their yards — children playing, women working in their gardens or just talking over the fences, men standing in groups talking or working on some project. They all stopped what they were doing and began to tease Earl the moment we came out of Theta's. "Take her arm now Earl. Ha-ha-ha. Don't they look nice? Treat her nice now. Look at Earl step. Ha-ha-ha. Have a good time." This went on until we had disappeared down the road. They all loved Earl, who was one of Inglewood's favorite young men. They wanted only the best for him so this teasing was just to show that they were happy for us. But this did not last long, for I soon learned that Earl was not really interested in one steady girl and had other girl friends in other villages. I was just added to all the others. He loved his freedom and he thought I was a little too young for him. I realized this would never amount to anything. I would never become Earl Jackson's wife even though I was head-over-heals in love with him. We went on dating though while I continued to work.

So, this was my life in Bridgetown... happy, sad, angry and unsure.

Downtown Bridgetown was a quaint little place. It looked

to me like the towns in western movies where a gunfight might break out at any moment. All the white folk seemed to know each other, and I could see they were beginning to know me as the little coloured girl who worked for the Joneses (not their real name). There were some small shops, one theater, a drug store, one restaurant and a post office. When I got my eight dollars' pay at the end of the week I loved to go to the drug store for an ice cream soda. My savings plan from the time I started to work was to put away five dollars a week. I had three dollars to spend, so I could go to a movie, buy some treats and a magazine, and even be able to take a treat up to Theta's boys. Eight dollars a week does not seem like much by today's standards but at that time it was a pretty good wage for a live-in maid. When I had saved enough, I was able to buy clothing. I was so proud when I was able to get myself a lovely new winter coat, one I really liked and did not have to settle for anything less.

The factory in Bridgetown closed and the men had to find work in other towns. Earl found work in Middleton, a small town nearby. He just came home on weekends, and though we still saw each other, we were not that close any longer. I enjoyed going by myself in the evenings to the only theater in town to see the movies. I was too shy to go walking down the aisle and would sit on the first seat I saw empty at the back. No one seemed to notice me. When I was going with Earl, we always sat up in the balcony and always on the left side. All of the Black young people sat up there. I supposed they liked it up there so they could smooch, so that was fine with me. But when I was alone I just sat in the first seat I saw. I came to find out later that the Black people sat up in the left balcony because they were not allowed to sit anywhere else. This small town was so prejudiced, the town was segregated. I don't know why they did not approach me when I did not go up in the balcony when I was alone but it was an accepted fact that the Black people at that time were not allowed to sit wherever they wished in this small theater.

This was a real shock to me, for in Weymouth all us young folk went to the one theater in town. We waited at the door for the theater to open, then we all crowded in and sat wherever we wanted to. This apparently had gone on in Bridgetown for years until Donald Clements came home from the war. He had been badly wounded, shot in the leg, and was using crutches. He walked into the theater one night and walked right down the middle aisle and sat right up front. It was not long before an usher came and asked him to move, to go and sit up in the balcony with the other coloured folk. They tell me that Donald stood up and said, "I have been all over Europe and been in many theaters much larger and greater than this and was never asked to sit in a special place for, as you say, coloured folk." The usher tried to quiet him but he would not stop. The usher went and got the manager but Donald went on, "I joined the army to protect my country and fought for all of you and nearly got my leg blown off in the war and to come back to find you people expect me to be treated like this? The people all over Europe treated us all with great respect and welcomed us everywhere we went, and here at home you tell me I can't sit where I like in this small town!" By now the lights were on and everyone sat quiet listening. When Donald finished his speech, he sat down and the show went on. Since then people could sit wherever they wanted in Bridgetown.

At first it did not seem strange to me if I had to wait a long time to be served when I went to the drug store for my weekly ice cream soda. I would have picked up my magazine and would be lost in it, not thinking the proprietor was ignoring me. It seems the druggist had told the man I was working for to "keep that little nigger maid out of" his store. Now it became clear to me why I always had to wait to be served when I went there for my soda treat. I had never ever imagined Bridgetown discriminated against Black people

In the meantime, some changes had come to Lottie's life.

Her beloved Jimmie was still confined to the sanitarium, though now he could come home on visits. He was being transferred to Camp Hill Hospital in Halifax. They decided to get married, bought a cute little home in Dartmouth and were able to be together on weekends. The wedding was wonderful, though sad and unusual, for they were married in the hospital. Again I was a bridesmaid and Lottie asked me to come to live with her in Dartmouth.

All the while I was having problems with my employers treting me badly, I was always complaining to Lottie and asking her what I could do. "Don't quit," she advised me, "you will never get another job in that small town or any other place in Nova Scotia if they learn you quit working for the great Joneses. But save your money, and when and if you want to come you are welcome." So I started seriously saving my money and waiting for the day when I had enough for my train fare and some money to last until I got work.

It was not long until I had saved enough money to go and live with Lottie in Dartmouth. I got a job and lived it up, dating two or three boys at a time. I was still very much in love with Earl Jackson but I did not have to have a house fall on me to know that the feeling was not mutual. So I was drowning my sorrows by living it up, working during the day and whenever I could, going out at night. It was fun in Dartmouth, there were lots of boys to choose from, and they all seemed interested in me, though I never got sexually involved, for I was very afraid of becoming pregnant. Some girl friends of mine had gotten pregnant and had taken their babies home to their mothers. I could not take my baby home to my mother so I was very careful not to be too promiscuous. But I lived it up, and at one point, I got very sick with measles and lost lots of weight. When I was well enough, I went on with my wild life.

The great thing about being in Dartmouth was that I spent a lot of time with Mae. She was married now but was still like a young girl. We had lots of fun together shopping and going over to Halifax to the movies and dances. We talked a lot and she told me many things I did not know. She was always telling me that I was pretty and looked good when I came all dressed up. It was nice to have someone tell me these things, especially a sister. I was her baby-sitter whenever she went out and I loved to be there with her lovely children. Mae was the same as she had been at home, fun, caring and a really understanding sister. Lottie was great too but still the strict one and was always upset with me whenever I was out late.

I don't really remember but I think she suggested that I go back to Bridgetown, so I don't think it was my idea alone to go back. I heard that Albert was home and looking for me and I was curious to find out what he looked like after three years. Lottie had gotten pretty tired of my wild ways and was happy when I had decided to go back to Bridgetown. When there, I sort of started seeing Earl again, I suppose for old time's sake, being careful not to let him see that I still loved him. I heard that Albert was home. He had been working in Sudbury, Ontario, for three years, had taken a leave of absence, and would be home for some time. I silently hoped I would see him, perhaps to apologize for treating him so badly at our last meeting. I had paid dearly for my behaviour and learned you can't make a person love you.

It was Harvest Supper time and everyone was going, so we all jumped into Earl's car and off we went to Weymouth to the Baptist Harvest Supper. Just like old times. I was so excited that I would be back, seeing my old girl friends, Loretta, Dorothy, Sylvia and many others, and after the supper we would all go down to the Vets Hangout and dance, dance, dance!

When Albert walked into the Church Hall, I was shocked. He had been working in the Nickel Mine in Sudbury, had gotten big and stocky, and had grown a mustache. He was dressed in a blue gabardine suit, his hair was black and curly, all the girls were hanging onto him, and he was showing off, with his pretty white teeth sparkling as he smiled. He looked directly at me when he came in. He must have felt me staring, walking through the crowd with all the girls hanging onto him, because he came right up to me. "Hi Chris, I was hoping to see you. I have a letter for you from your brother Bernard. Will you be going to Harold's hall, the Vets Hangout?" I was only able to nod my head, "Yes." "Well, I will go home and get the letter and bring it to you there. See you there then," and off he went with all the girls hanging on and disappeared in the crowd, leaving me breathless.

All the young people had crowded into the Vets Hangout and it was the same as ever. Although three years had passed, we all danced the same jive, and it was just super to be dancing there again. I spotted "Poppy" (Darryl Smith) coming across the floor, knowing he was coming to dance with me. I loved to dance with Poppy, he seemed to have six legs when he did the boogie-woogie and I loved it when I saw him coming from away across the floor. He would be grinning from ear to ear, his body jumping to the beat of the music, and did we dance... his long legs flying over my head and everywhere. It was not long before Albert walked in the door, and in no time, we were swinging to the oldies. He told me he had been working with Bernard and gave me the letter he had brought from him, and we continued to dance most of the night.

Now Earl starts to hang around. Usually he would not dance at all until the last dance, which would be a slow one, and then we could go home, but tonight he was all over me whenever he got a chance. When brother Guy saw me he nearly flipped, "You are too skinny, Christie, you need some rest. Why don't you stay here at home with Grace and me. You look awful, all drug out..." Guy was like that — would tell you like it is, never holding anything back — and he was right, I was tired. I knew I needed some rest as I had been running wild and was tired of it all. Now that Guy had said it, I knew I just wanted to stop and get a grip on myself. Guy continued, "If you go on like this you will end up with T.B. or something. You look like a skeleton, so thin." Guy said he and Grace had been talking about it and they both agreed with the idea of my staying with them awhile.

To stay at home in Weymouth for a while sounded very good to me, so right there and then I accepted, and right away I felt better. When I told Earl I was staying home for a while he looked shocked and asked me to go outside with him to talk, "I love you Chris," he said, "don't stay away from me." This was the only time he had said he loved me... too late... I had already been hurt enough by him. I think he saw the sparks from the kindles starting to relight in the eyes of Albert and me.

That fall and winter leading to Christmas were great. Guy, Grace, Albert and I had more than fun together. I learnt that Guy and Albert had been good friends before the war and called each other companions. Because Guy was always staying with Aunt Gert, I never knew who his boyhood friends were. So when Guy lied about his age and joined the Army, Albert started being friends with Frankie, though he was older than Frankie.

The letter Albert had brought supposedly from Bernard was really from his wife, Ruth. Bernard had, at one time, visited me at the Joneses' home to see how I was making out. I had not heard from him after that. Lottie or someone must have been telling him of me and what sort of life I was leading, and asked for his advice, and yes, I had heard that Bernard was somewhere in Ontario. I thought he was in the forest somewhere, always the woodsman.

So here was this lady I had never met, asking me to come to Sudbury and visit or stay with her and Bernard. She said she could use my company because Bernard worked the night shift. Her letter was wonderful, very inviting, and she did not even know me.

Albert and I were like two young teenagers again that fall and winter, walking through the snow, going down on the ice pond. Albert could skate very well but I could only watch. We had not owned skates as children, but it was fun when I borrowed Gracie's skates and he tried to teach me. Albert's leave of absence was up in January, so he had to go back to Sudbury. "I wish you would come with me, Chris, and as soon as I have worked awhile and saved more money we can get married. I have never stopped loving you, Chris, and I want to take care of you. I don't ever want you to have to go to work again. You were never cut out to do that hard work. Sudbury is very cold though at this time of the year, and there won't be much for you to do, but you know you can stay with Bernard, and his wife Ruth is a very nice person." Albert went on to say, "Chris, I know you don't love me as I do you but love can grow, and in time you will learn to love at least our relationship, and I will try and make you happy. The wages that are paid by INCO in Sudbury are very good and we can live very well on my income. You will never have to work again."

Now to this girl, at the time, that sounded real good. Just imagine... Albert and me in a great new world, starting all over again. He was not aware of my true feelings, not knowing I was seeing him in a new light. He had grown into a man now, a responsible man, who wanted to take on the responsibility of a wife. And I had also done some growing and learning about the world and needed to settle down. The thought of getting married, to me, meant children, and children was what I wanted most of all.

The times I spent with Theta, Mae and Guy's children were the happiest times of my life. I was really envious of them, having these wonderful little smart people, and could not be with them enough, to listen to them talk in their cute baby voices and try to sing, and to watch them play and to hold them in my arms. The thought of having some of my own was very exciting, so my imagination took off, and I was sitting in a home in Sudbury with a baby on my lap and one playing on the floor. That picture was enough to convince me to accept Albert's offer, that and the fact that I was somewhat in love with him. Something about the way he wanted to take over my life appealed to me. I thought I needed just that, someone to care and do for me. I had been spoiled as a child and I thought I wanted that again. I did not know at the time just how much Albert wanted to take over my life.

Guy and Grace were very happy when we broke the news to them; this was what they had been hoping for. Albert had convinced Guy to come also to Sudbury to work in the mines; they were not hiring on workers then but would be in the spring. So Guy would come then, and when he got settled would send for Grace and the children. The four of us would sit in their little house and discuss all these plans during the rest of the fall and winter leading to Christmas.

It was Christmas Eve. And what a Christmas! The three children — Hope, Ria and Sheldon — made Christmas perfectly exciting. Guy was a perfect Santa Claus and even went outside to make a noise as if it was Santa coming to convince the children to go to bed. Albert came loaded down with gifts for all, and of course, there was a big Christmas dance at the Vets Hangout.

Life in Ontario

We arrived in Sudbury around 10 p.m. The weather had gradually turned colder the farther north we got. It had taken us three days to travel from Weymouth — Albert, his brother Wilbert (who was on his way to Toronto to visit relatives and, hopefully, find work), and myself. It had been an exciting trip. Wilbert and I were glued to the window the whole way, taking in the acres and acres of farmland; cities with great, tall buildings; factories; harbours with large ships; sights neither of us had seen before. Albert, who had already travelled this way, was quick to point out sights of interest — showing off — thinking he knew everything. Same old Albert. After meeting with their brother and sister, who were at the Toronto Station to meet us, and having just a short time to visit with Bob and Gloria, Albert and I had to rush to catch the train that would continue on to Sudbury.

I had experienced cold weather back in Nova Scotia but never anything as cold as this. We had not long disembarked from the train when frost had gathered on our heads, eyelashes and upper lips. It was even stinging our faces. There was a gray fog of frost in the air and my once neatly combed and styled hair was standing straight out, clumps of hair slapping me in the face. I remember thinking, I want to get on the first train out of here and go back home.

Albert had retrieved our luggage and started to walk, yelling back to me, "Come on!" his long strides causing me to run. "Bernard lives just up on Notre Dame, not far," he said. Can't we take a taxi or a bus or something to get out of this cold, I am thinking as I stumble through the snow and cold, trying to keep up. After what seemed like a very long walk, we arrived at Bernard's and the welcome was great! He swung open the door with a big grin and pulled us into his lovely, comfortable home.

This Bernard was very different from the brother I had known, in every way. He was paler and much slimmer, better-looking than I had remembered. He had a big friendly smile that I had not seen much of. Into the room walked this lovely lady and I'm thinking, How in the hell did Bernard get this beautiful woman to marry him? Ruth was stunning! She reminded me of Lauren Bacall or Veronica Lake (movie stars of that era) and now she was repeating the words of the letter she had sent me... "I am so glad you came. It is so lonely around here with Bernard working the afternoon shift." She proceeded to show us around, pointing out a room that Albert would use upstairs, and for me, a cozy room off the kitchen. She soon had us all eating a lovely hot dinner with hot drinks around her table.

Albert, Bernard and Ruth got into a conversation about Sudbury and mining. Still being very shy, I kept quiet but both Bernard and Ruth kept me in the conversation, asking me about myself, commenting on my looks and appearance. I was surprised to hear Bernard complimenting me, for I had always had in my mind the memory of him saying he did not care what happened to me — he had only been worried about Frankie. This had put a rift between Frankie and me as I had resented the fact that Frankie was able to stay at home and I had to go.

That winter was both fun and romantic. When the men had time off, the four of us would walk all over the town of Sudbury, with them showing me all the interesting things — like the big nickel coin that had been erected on one of the many mountains. It seemed like everything belonged to the International Nickel Company (INCO). I though this was great. There was a school, hospital, entertainment centre, and clinic, all belonging to INCO. It was a lovely place to bring up children. I was told that the children born there were called INCO children. That was fine with me, for more than anything I wanted to raise children.

Ruth and I spent long hours together as the men worked the afternoon shift, three until twelve. It did not take us long to get to know each other. She taught me how to play cribbage, so we sat most evenings talking and playing crib. Now I had a sister-in-law and friend.

I tasted my first beer the night they took me to a tavern. I liked the taste of it then, and it is still my favourite beverage. It felt strange to be in a tavern, and even more strange to be in a tavern with my brother Bernard. I shall always remember the compliment I received from him after we arrived home and were relaxing around the table. Bernard looked me straight in the eye and said, "I was proud of you tonight, Christie. You carried yourself like a lady. You walked right in the place with your head up and drank your drink like a lady. I am very proud of you." He will never know how much it meant to hear him say that to me after all this time, and I thought, Bernard does like me.

Albert and I got married on July 14, 1950. There were only twelve guests at our wedding but it was very nice. We took a little apartment near Bernard and Ruth.

After Sudbury had blustered and blown a cold hard winter, it broke out into a beautiful warm spring and summer. This brought many more Black people to Sudbury because of the availability of work at the INCO mines, including my brother Guy, who sent for his wife and children as soon as he was settled. They arrived in time to help with my wedding. It was so nice to have Guy and Grace with us again. Then came Mae and her husband and family, and Frankie came with them. I was so happy to have Frankie in the same place with me again and we soon began taking long walks around Sudbury, just reminiscing. Ruth, Mae and Grace were all expecting, and when they got together, all the talk was of their children and the new ones on the way. They were all very good mothers, which is what I wanted to be.

So life in Sudbury was full. Our men were making very good money. Most of the people there were very friendly, and it seemed that everyone there was on the same income level, what with all the men working in the mines. Mae, Grace and Ruth had children every year but I still did not become pregnant.

A terrible tragedy took place that came as a shock to everyone. Mae's husband, Victor, was accidentally killed, leaving Mae with five children to look after. It was devastating! He was so young and was just beginning to make a nice home for Mae and the children. We all tried to help in any way that we could. Sudbury was not the same to me after that though, so when Albert suggested we move to Toronto, I agreed to go. He had gone to visit his siblings there once when we had one of our many breakups, and he thought a new start in a new place would be good for us.

"We are not getting along very well here, and I would like to get out of the mining," he said. This was a very dangerous job. Many things had happened underground that would frighten even the toughest man. Albert had seen his partner get killed when a large rock fell on him, so he was not too happy about going down in the mine each day. My happiness in Sudbury was not what I had hoped for. I still had no children and had given up hope of ever having one.

We stayed with Albert's sister Gloria in Toronto until we found work, then found two rooms on the second floor of a rooming house. This was a great learning experience for me as there were couples from all walks of life there in the large rooming house run by a very nice couple, Al and Eva Gelfand. They kept the house nice and clean and got along well with all the tenants. Eva was a pretty little lady, and it was plain to see that all the tenants liked and respected her.

We soon learned that the owner of the place did not want Black people living there, but Eva rented to whoever she wanted to. The owner came around on Saturday afternoons to collect the rents so Eva just told us to stay in our rooms until he had gone and then things would go on as usual, with everyone roaming the halls, going into each other's rooms, all making friends. There were prostitutes, gay men and women, Black and White couples, but everyone minded their own business.

The Gelfands had two pretty little girls — Denise and Lorraine — and soon Eva was expecting another. I was very happy again, and with both of us working there did not seem to be time for Albert and I to get into fights. We spent lots of time with Al and Eva.

I noticed that I was beginning to feel sick, so when I told my sister-in-law Gloria, she sent me to her doctor, who said after some examinations, "Well, you are just fine and the baby is about six weeks along." Well, I was so shocked that I just started to cry. The doctor said, "Oh, don't be so upset. This has happened to many young girls and if you need some advice from me then we can talk." I controlled myself long enough to say, "I'm not crying because I'm worried. I have been married for four years and never became pregnant. Thank you, Doctor. I am very happy." Albert was, at that time, working close enough to come home for lunch, so I told him then about the good news of my pregnancy. Back on his job, when he was thinking about this fact, he nearly cut his finger off with the saw he was using.

When Al and Eva had saved enough to buy a home, they asked us to come with them and we rented the third-floor flat in their home. It was a cute place with enough room for a little nursery for the baby, and on April 24th my baby girl was born prematurely. She was not due until June and was tiny. She had to stay in the hospital until she gained more weight. It was so hard to come home and leave my beautiful little daughter there for two weeks. Albert was proud to call himself "the milkman" as he had to take my milk to the hospital each morning and night for the baby. Soon it was time to bring her home.

Albert threw a big party and all the relatives and friends came, but I just wanted to stay in her room and stare at my lovely little brown girl. She was like a chocolate doll, with shining black hair and brown eyes that crinkled at the corners, just like Albert's. I just could not believe that this little doll was really mine and I became afraid that I would not be able to look after properly. What if I dropped her? I was both happy and frightened as a new mother.

Albert had applied for a job as a porter on the railroad and soon he was working for C.P.R. He looked so nice in his uniform and proved to be a good porter. He got on very well with the passengers and children who rode on the train. People would even ask him to look out for their children if they had to send them alone on the train. He received many letters of commendation.

Albert had a great personality; he loved to tease and joke with people. He had the route from Toronto to Winnipeg, six days away and three days at home. It would have been lonely if not for Eva, her children and my baby. Eva and I both named my little girl. I had always liked the name Theresa and Eva suggested Marie for her middle name. So she became Theresa Marie Cromwell.

Eva had a boy, Roger, in March, making him just a month older than Theresa. The two of them played together and we took them shopping together, the two of them in one carriage. We got a lot of stares from passersby. A Black baby and a White baby together in one carriage was quite a sight in those days (1954/55). Eva and I loved to add to the shocking sight by her carrying Theresa and me carrying Roger. Once, when they were playing together, he took Theresa by the hem of her shirt and was making her walk. This was such a cute sight, and to this day Roger always tells Theresa that he taught her how to walk. She always replies, "And that's why I walk so funny." Our families have remained good friends.

I banged my knee once and had to be hospitalized for a time so Eva kept Theresa for us. She told me that they had taken all of the children for a routine Sunday drive, with their girls in the back and Roger in the car seat. Eva was holding Theresa on her lap and there were many near-crashes when other cars would pass and see Eva holding a Black baby. (Those were the days.)

Albert and I longed to have more children, and soon after Theresa turned six, we were blessed with another child. I named her Deborah. Albert and I loved children; we didn't just want to have just one. And when Deborah came into our lives, we knew we wanted to have more. I remember the day she came home — Theresa placed all her toys around her, in an attempt to share. Deborah was so close to her sister Theresa, always following her everywhere she went.

Deborah was very pretty and was such a little lady. She had big beautiful eyes with bouncy black curls in her hair. We didn't have much money back then so I had to sew clothing for the children. Deborah loved to dress up in the dresses I made for her. When she was a little girl, she was quite shy, but she grew up to be a very courageous young woman.

Not long after Deborah came into our lives, we were blessed with my only son, Alan. I love boys, always have, and was so excited to finally have the opportunity to raise a son. He was so cute and small when he came home, such a happy baby too. He loved to play and joke around and always kept me busy. Both Deborah and Theresa looked after him; all three of my children were very close. He truly looked up to his two older sisters and they both loved him dearly. I was so blessed to have my two girls and my son. I always dreamed of having a large family of my own just like I had during my own childhood.

Albert also had a large family. He had nine brothers and

sisters and all but one were living in Toronto. It was nice to have his family so close. We all got together as often as possible and their parents came often from Nova Scotia to visit. They were all great Christians, although Albert and I only attended church occasionally. Albert was always very close to his siblings, and when his brother Foster was to be baptized, we just had to go to the church for the occasion. At the end of the service, when shaking hands with Albert, the minister, Rev. McMillen, said to him, "You do remember what to wear to the baptism Sunday?" Well, Albert was so dumb-founded he just said, "Ah, ah, yes, Sir."

"Very well," the minister went on to say, "The baptism will be right after church so be sure to bring a change of clothing." And the minister went on and on about the fact that Albert was to be baptized that coming Sunday.

We had previously been asked out to the home of friends, and naturally, there were going to be alcoholic drinks served. However Albert flatly refused to take a drink, and he just sat with his head down most of the day and kept repeating, "Why did the minister think I was to be baptized?" We all tried to tell him that the minister must have gotten him mixed up with someone else but this didn't seem to sink in. He just continued to sit, looking very upset and in great wonderment.

That Monday was the start of his three days off and he disappeared early that morning. I supposed that he had gone to visit one of the family, or perhaps a friend, and would be home much later. When he got home he told me that he had gone back to the church to wait for the minister to show up and he could explain that he was not the man who was to be baptized. They talked and talked, and Albert decided he would be baptized after all. He added, "Please Christie, would you come and be baptized with me?" Naturally, I was more than shocked. My first thought was to say, "No, I'm not ready for this. I still like to dance, have a drink, sing songs, read good books," but the look on Albert's face made me stop and think again. I listened to all he had to say, and one of the things he said was that the minister would come to the house to talk to me.

Well, Rev. McMillen shot down all my excuses. "You can dance," he said. "David danced," and he read me the scripture. "Jesus drank wine, even made a special wine at a wedding," and he read to me that scripture. "You can continue to read good books. There are many exciting love stories in the Bible. God loves you and wants you to become His child and grow in grace."

And so, at the next baptism we were baptized together at First Baptist Church. Albert, for the first time, brought me material, white satin, to make a dress to be baptized in. This began a complete change in our lives. We both had the desire to become good Christians. Rev. McMillen told us that we do not become a different person, or a great Christian, the minute we are baptized, but that we become a child of God, and then we grow in grace and become stronger and learn as we continue to study and begin to know God as our loving Saviour.

Our daughter Theresa was now growing into a lovely little lady and was very happy to be going to church. Her cousins were going so she looked forward to Sunday mornings. She got to know and love the Rev. and Mrs. McMillen and decided to call the minister, "Rev. Daddy."

Soon they all had started school in an area where there were no other Black children. I suppose they got some strange looks and questions, which they seemed to have handled in their own way.

Theresa wanted to do things on her own and did not want me to walk her to school, so I consented to let her go by herself. I walked behind her, hiding behind trees, hedges and bushes. Deborah was a little on the shy side and spent more time with me; she helped me with her younger brother. She would walk him to school and play with him a lot. She also followed Theresa around. There were always lots of children hanging around the house. Theresa would gather her friends around to play Peter Pan. Theresa was always Peter Pan and I think Deborah was Tinker Bell or perhaps she had to pretend to be a lost boy. I'm not sure if Deborah liked pretending to be a boy very much but she would do anything for her big sister.

Alan on the other hand was always off somewhere playing with the other boys in the neighbourhood. He was very active and fun loving. I remember there was a time when a white woman who owned a store on our street called my son Alan a mean name. I marched down to that store and proceeded to tell that woman what was what. Other kids picked on my children often, but I taught them to be proud of who they were no matter what anyone else said. When the time came for parents' night, Theresa's teacher asked me when my husband and I had moved here from Africa. It seems that the children had all gathered around Theresa at school and were asking her why she was Black. She proceeded to tell them that she was from Africa, her father was an African king, and she was a princess who owned a lion while living in Africa.

Our lives were complete. We had a church, a home, three lovely children. Rev. McMillen wanted Albert to be able to work more with him as he had plans for him to become one of his deacons. Albert found a new job in the city, working at the Y.M.C.A. He also arranged for us to move into the apartment above the parsonage — a large, lovely place. I was still in the habit of tucking the children into bed each night, and I started reading them stories from the Bible. Little did they know that I was learning the Bible at the same time.

It was not long before Albert, his brother Foster and the other men were to become deacons, and would, in time, be ordained deacons. They all became a great help to the Reverend and the church. I wanted to go to work but Albert would not hear of it, and I must admit, I did not want to leave my children with anyone.

After Albert and I left Sudbury we did not have much time to miss the loved ones we had left there, for they often came to us or we went to visit them. We had not been in Toronto too long when Frankie decided to visit. It was wonderful to have him there. He became Pappy to Theresa, and indeed, he was like a second father to her. Naturally, Frankie and I took long walks together, spending lots of time reminiscing. Mae and her children also came, and as they grew old enough to travel alone, the children would come to spend summer vacations with us. Albert was just thrilled with this, for their father, Victor, had been his very good friend in Sudbury and he wanted to do whatever he could for those children. Though Albert tried to be a very strict uncle, he spoiled them some and loved having them, so our home was always full of relatives. And we loved it!

By this time we had moved into a house with a rent-to-buy option, and we had amble space to accommodate visiting relatives. We always got a big laugh when, each spring, we would get a letter from one of Mae's children, "Dear Aunt Christie and Uncle Albert..." Here we go again.

Our home was always crowded with young people as many of our nieces and nephews came from Nova Scotia and Sudbury and stayed with us, either when looking for work or to further their education. Albert and I both loved having them all around. Our families continued to visit each other. Lottie was now married to a new man, Coulter States. Her Jimmy did not live long though he fought a long, hard battle with tuberculosis. Lottie and Coulter would come from Dartmouth, Theta and James from Bridgetown, Guy and Grace from Sudbury, and Mae always came as well. There was lots and lots of laughter in the house and it always took me back to my youth. We would go off to Sudbury in the car to spend many happy vacations there with the folks, and we would also visit the relatives in Nova Scotia.

Our church was growing, with many young people, as well as the faithful old folk who had been there from the beginning and could tell you many stories of what went on back then. Albert was well liked by the senior ladies;

they all spoke so well of him. He showed them respect but would tease them all. Many times I would see him being very helpful to them, ushering them up the front steps and to their seats, and then suddenly he would jump back to avoid being hit by a purse, umbrella, book, anything they had in hand, and Albert would hurry away laughing. He would have said something to them that would make them want to hit him, but then they settled in their seats, shaking with laughter. We had formed the singing group, The Gospel Chorus. This was great fun. We went all over the place singing, even to some parts of the U.S.

By now, Albert had taken on a new job (that paid more money), at Singers Lighting Company, as the head spray-painter. This job is what he wanted for some time, to get good pay so that he wouldn't have to worry about his income, although working with lacquer all the time was not good, so I was told. He had to be in a small room and spray lamp parts before they were assembled. One should only work about five years with lacquer, then get away from it. Some time earlier Albert had developed an ulcer and his doctor had prescribed medication for it.

Albert and I went off to Nova Scotia on vacation and found each other all over again. We were back in Weymouth, where it all started, just the two of us in a big, beautiful new car in which we ran all over Nova Scotia. We had been married twenty-five years and had sent out invitations to all to come to an anniversary party to be held on the 14th of July. We had a wonderful vacation and found ourselves making love in all the old familiar places, driving all over Nova Scotia, visiting all the family and old friends. When visiting Everett and his family in Birchtown, Shelburne County, we told them we were looking to buy a house, so Elizabeth (Everett's wife) took us around to look at houses. We found a lovely ranch house and decided to take it. So our plans were settled — we would retire soon and move back home to a nice eight-room house on forty acres of land in Nova Scotia. The children would come with us, or not. We would leave the home in Toronto there for them, and we would have a place to stay when we visited. How wonderfully perfect everything was turning out for all concerned!

Back in Weymouth again the anniversary party was a wonderful success, with all the family there.

It is now a Saturday morning in August. Albert had worked all morning, come home at noon, ate a lunch in the living room, and as usual, leaned back in his lazy-boy chair. Theresa and her friend Cyril came in just then from shopping. Cyril joined Albert and as they started a conversation, I joined Theresa in the kitchen. Cyril called to me, "Mom! Something is wrong with Albert!" Walking into the living room I could see he was making a snoring noise and his body was twitching. "Oh, he always does that in his sleep," I said as I shook him. "Hey, Albert, wake up." But the sounds and the twitching were getting worse. I was trying to revive him as Theresa came in and pushed me away. Taking over, she started mouth-to-mouth resuscitation. I rushed to call 9-1-1. After what seemed like hours, the ambulance came.

Albert had suffered a massive heart attack. A blood clot had traveled through his artery to his heart, completely blowing it up. Albert would not pull through, Albert would not live. I find it very hard to describe this terrible shocking time; I can only try to describe my feelings. Anger, I was very angry, angry at Albert. He knew better than to continue to do things that would destroy his body. Then there was disbelief. This could not be. Albert could not die, he was too strong, too powerful. I was supposed to die first! So many things went rushing through my head. The children and I can't go on without him. The first people I thought of calling when in the hospital waiting room were Al and Eva Gelfand. Al came right away and remained with me all during the time, pumping coffee into me.

I hated it when people said that this was *the will of God*. God does not *will* people to destroy their bodies by putting things into them that are not good for them. This was *not* God's will.

How do I describe my life after that? I continued to work, talk, eat and sleep. But I was numb, and I think, still angry; confused; meeting men with only one thing on their mind. I have watched the birds flying around in circles as if they don't know where to go. I was like them. I went to work, I ate, I slept, and I existed. I found that a good drink of vodka kept me from thinking. Then I found myself drinking every night, whenever I was alone. I could have become an alcoholic quite easily. I believe Theresa saved me by asking me to quit my job and babysit for her. This began my daycare job.

When I was with my grandchildren, I would not drink. Then friends of Theresa's asked if I could take their children, and women I met at the school when picking up the children asked me if I could take their children. I ended up with eleven children, aged from four to fourteen, and what a lovely group of children they were! I guess in a way I did have one big family.

Sarah and Joshua — redheads. Joshua was just four years old when I got him. I looked after him until he was fourteen. My love, my son, Joshua. Sarah — a young lady who helped me with the menu planning and controlling the younger ones, Tasha and Tony. They were brother and sister whose Trinidadian parents became my good friends. Richard, oh Richard — how frightened you were of this Black lady when you first came. But we became great friends, and even when you grew up, you always came back to visit. Coleman, who came as a baby, would hide his glasses when he knew his mother was coming to take him home. We always wondered why. Did he just want to stay longer? Sarah and Tony, whose parents were German, were a great help to me in many ways. And of course, my grandchildren, Thomas, Nicolle and CJ (Theresa's children) and much later for a short time I looked after my third grandson Amadeus, who looked so much like his mother

Deborah.

I had worked many jobs but this was the best. I was my own boss and I made very good money. I spent most of it travelling when my vacation came in July and August, and also on the Christmas party I gave them each year, just before the holidays. These children were like my own. During the day, I took all eleven to and from school, pushing a carriage or stroller with the little ones in it. I did this four times a day. It was great fun and I forgot about myself, about my anger, my drinking and my loneliness. I was too tired come night to sit and brood.

A neighbour, who was eighty-nine years old at the time, told me that she had lost her husband when she was about my age. She told me that the shock never goes completely away. It will get easier, but it will always come back to you and it will still be like a shock. It will seem as though it just happened. It will be as if you are living it all over again, but each time it will be easier to bear. She was so right. It always comes back, and it is still a big shock.

My only problem with having the daycare was getting rid of the parents in the evening. They would all come to pick up their children, then stay for the evening talking. They got to know each other so they would sit in my kitchen and have tea and talk and talk and talk. I could never get rid of them, but oh, how I loved those evenings.

Most of the children come back to visit me. They are all grown up and have good positions. Only Joshua has not come back. He says he cannot, he is afraid he may cry. He and I were so close.

I cannot complete my story without including Leonard Blenman, a man I met when I was going through my empty life and was spending it lonely and drinking to forget. This man was different. He did not drink, just loved life, and he loved to travel. He and I travelled through most of Canada and the U.S. We both loved music so we drove in big cars and listened to music. He was a great friend. He helped me in a lot of ways to get through, and on cold winter days when the children and I would come out of school, Leonard's car waiting to take us all home was a welcome sight. He was always there to help me and shall always and forever be my friend.

All of my children are working and are on their own. Deborah, who has changed her name to Ericha, gave me a wonderful little grandson, Amadeus. She grew into a lovely woman. She always says she is like me in many ways. I am so proud of her; she worked her way through school, graduated from Ryerson University and now has her very own business — a tea room called LaTeaDa in the beaches right on Queen Street. It is the most beautiful place and I know she loves it.

My son Alan has a great job. He is a youth worker and loves working with delinquent boys and girls, and gets on well with the other staff. The children think the world of him. He is a great son and we have great times together when we can. He is happy-go-lucky and doesn't take life too seriously; he's lots of fun. He always calls me on my birthday and sings me silly songs. We love to play cards together for hours at a time.

The first of my grandchildren (I have four) was Thomas Albert Augustan. I will always remember Albert and I awaiting his birth, sitting in the waiting room saying that we were really not ready for this. But, ready or not, here he came. So cute, with damp straight hair. When I held him he looked up at me with such sad eyes, as if to say, "I need someone to love me." When I look at Thomas, to this day, I can still see that sad look of wanting to be loved.

Nicolle Evenly Lorraine, my little girl. She is all girl now, a grown-up lady. I always called her Lady Jane, those big expressive eyes, always so inquisitive, wanting to know everything, always listening so intently to all I told her but never doing as she was told. She and I have shared so much. How lovely it is to talk to your grandchildren about everything and anything, to laugh, dance, sing and yes, cry. I found it to be such fun when I was asked to babysit them.

Come bedtime I would tuck them in after a story and say, "Now go to sleep. I don't want to hear a peep out of you," and as I'm leaving the room I would always hear them say, "Peep."

Then there were days of waiting at the subway for them, hoping they would not get lost or something, then the excited relief when I would see them come running, straight into my open arms. And now they are all grown up and I can ask them for advice.

Amadeus Markes Cromwell is my daughter Ericha's son, and what a man he is. He is very handsome, with his mother's good looks. He would come and visit me often, so sweet and loving and very smart. I think he should work in TV or the movies; he would make a great actor. I remember when he was born, so small and cute. Ericha is such a great mother; she always took real good care of her son. Before she had Amadeus, she helped Theresa with her three children all the time, taking them to Ontario Place and buying them all kinds of toys and treats. I guess that prepared her for motherhood in the best way.

Alan was a wonderful uncle to his nieces and nephews; I have three great-grandchildren — Shamaia, Jordon, Chantaya, Nicolle's children, and Thomas' son Isaiah Christopher, named after me. "Fabulous" is the only way to describe them, and "very smart," as the children are today. The three older grandchildren call Alan Candy Man because he always brings them candy.

Cyril James (CJ) John Cromwell Simmonds, the one for whom I write this, is, as I've already stated, the one who is very close to me, for he has been with me most of his young life.

Though I looked after all eleven children all day, until school vacations, I had CJ with me all the time, so he and I had lots of time together to go exploring parks and areas of Toronto that we had not seen before. It was hard not to think of him as my child. I would even bring him along when I vacationed in Nova Scotia. I love all my grandchildren, but

CJ and I have always been the closest. We lived very near to each other so I was always going to visit them: Theresa and her new husband Cyril and CJ, who always came to meet me ever since he was a young boy. His father Cyril just loves to barbeque and have people over for a big feast, so it was not unusual for Cyril to phone and ask me to come down for a good meal on any afternoon. CJ, as usual, would come to meet me. I stepped out of the door and CJ said, "That's a nice dress you're wearing. You look nice, Gramma."

"Do you have company?" I asked. "If anyone is there I am not going in." He said, "No,", as we walked along, until we got to the gate, then said, "except Uncle Neville. He is here." By that time, it was too late for me to turn around and go back the way I had come. In the back yard, we found Cyril and Neville Simmonds. I had heard of Neville from Cyril many times. Cyril's uncle, who was now a widower, had lost his wife after a long illness. Neville had cared for his wife for some years and now he was alone. Cyril had often said that he thought Neville and I should get together. I had met him before at Cyril's mother's birthday party and I thought then that he seemed like a nice man. Now after the big barbeque dinner, we had a chance to sit and talk and I found him a very nice person to talk to. He was also very handsome, about two inches taller than me, stocky build, lovely chocolate complexion, graying hair, a smile that lights up his whole face, and eyes that seem to see right through to your very soul. He is from St. Kitt's but has an English accent, very well-spoken. We had a wonderful conversation there on Theresa and Cyril's porch. He drove me home and we spent the rest of that summer getting to know each other and falling in love.

Life in St. Kitts

It is 5:30 a.m. — I am sitting on the front porch watching the sun come up over Bird Rock, which is a small mountain. I look to my right and there is a pink horizon announcing the arrival of the sun. The pretty lights of Basseterre are like many Christmas trees, and the sounds of the animals — barking, honking, crowing, mooing — make a lovely song. Neville says they are all thanking God for another day. I see an egret flying low across the mountain on my left following a cow. They love to ride on the cows and pick the parasites (ticks) off. The cows welcome the egret.

Soon, down the road will come many sheep and goats. Neville tells me that their owner just lets them out and away they go, all day grazing wherever they wish. When evening comes we can see them returning home. I look forward to seeing all the people walking by. Although most drive cars, many still walk into town, which is just a twenty-minute walk from here. The children, so clean and pretty in their uniforms, all seem very happy, some singing as they pass along.

The temperature here is very hot but the trade winds from the Caribbean Sea and the Atlantic Ocean together send a breeze over the Island. Here on the porch

Christie in St. Kitts

115

I have a lovely view of the deep-water port where some ships come in; others go to Port Zante. Later, I see a large cruise ship glide slowly into the harbour, where all the taxi drivers are awaiting their turn to drive the tourists to the many beaches, or else around the Island. Neville is among them, waiting his turn. He loves to show off his Island. He worked for many years in Canada but now that he is retired he is able to do what he likes, and this is what he loves to do.

We got married on May the 29th in 2002. Much to everyone's surprise, we did not want a big wedding. Both he and I have big families, and as Neville said, we wanted a marriage, not a wedding. The only ones present were my oldest daughter Theresa and her husband, Neville's oldest daughter and her husband, who performed the ceremony, and their daughter. It was just a coincidence that they were in Toronto on business at the time. It was a wonderful ceremony and I could not ask for a better husband. We live here for part of the year, then go back to Canada for the other part. I love St. Kitt's and hope to spend my remaining days here.

Thanks be to God. When I left Nova Scotia to venture out into the world I was uneducated, lacking in knowledge about many facts of life and had a chip on my shoulder. I found it hard at first to grow accustomed to being friends with White people. In Sudbury we all associated with everyone, for most of the men worked for INCO. We were all friends there — we partied together and visited each other's homes. I am sure there were some prejudiced people and unrest going on — but not that I experienced. Toronto was a different story. One could feel the prejudice, the bigotry, there, though it was very subtle. I worked in many fields there and most of the jobs at that time had mostly White workers, so being Black on the job was an experience! I got a kick out of them when they would start a conversation with me by saying, "I like Sammy Davis Jr.," and I would always say, "Oh, I can't stand him," and walk away. (I really do love Sammy though.) I always got asked if it was true that Black men are well-endowed, and I would put a look of utter satisfaction on my face and answer, "Oh, yes!"

I found that the European people were very good to work with. They were not interested in what you looked like, but how well you did your job. I have worked for days, months, years with some Europeans and the subject of race was never mentioned. We did our work, went for breaks or lunches together, had lots of laughs and got along very well, never getting too personal, which was fine with me.

I recall one nice woman from Holland. Since she had been on the job for years, she was showing me the work, and we had gotten into many arguments and disagreements while she was training me. After about two weeks, when I finally got it right and was doing a perfect job, she gave me a look of utter disgust and said, "Do you know that you are brown?"

"Oh no! Am I?" From that day on, we remained the best of friends.

My children had to go through lots of troubles at school but they handled it their way. Theresa had to sit in the classroom and listen to the story of Little Black Sambo, and when the words Little Black Sambo were read by the teacher, all the children would turn and look at her. Theresa had her way of handling all of it and she turned out to be a lovely person who has the love of God, and Jesus is her personal friend.

I suppose having to care for children of all races and getting to know and love them gave me a love for all peoples.

Why do I love Christmas and believe in Santa Claus? Well, I had more than love from all nine of my siblings, they were Santa — supportive, caring, comforting, loving and understanding throughout my life, and Christmas, to me, was every day.

Weymouth Falls reunion, Front: Harold, Theta, Irving, Mae, Frankie; Back: Everett, Guy, Lottie, Bernard, Christie

Bernard's 80th birthday, Weymouth Falls, Back: Irving, Harold, Bernard, Frankie, Guy, Everett; Front: Christie, Mae, Lottie, Theta

Sept /22/84

Hi EVERETT

I was visiting with Mae in Prince George B.C. in Aug. She is well.

She let me read this poem. she had written one night when she was lonely and thinking of you Brothers. I thought you would get a kick out of reading it.

I think it is price less.

so here it is.

by the way - I am fine and hope this note will find you all the same.

yours with Love.

Sister Christie

Following is the above-mentioned poem, written by sister Mae ...

CRACK A LIMB ACROSS YOUR KNEE

Memories in thoughts
Thoughts into words
So here's a little memory
I hope you don't get bored
It's mostly pertaining to brothers
Bear with me and you will see
Think of the many times you had to
"Crack a limb across your knee"

Did you ever think of the "good ol' days" —
You came runnin' from the head of the field?
You felt so hot and sticky
You thought you were going to feel
You want to do something daring
You jump up and hit the mat on the line
You better not stop too quickly
There are five more coming behind

Just now you would like to venture outside
Play ball — raid a garden — steal a few peas
When you hear the voice coming from inside
"Crack some limbs across your knees!"

You just got your back off the wall
To get going on your stilts
You think perhaps she's busy inside
Maybe workin' on some quilts
Your buddies are strollin' down the road
You are showin' off, indeed
When you hear a voice from inside —
"Crack a limb across your knee!"

Think of the berry-pickin'
Through the hot sun and bushes, you wish
You were that lucky grasshopper
Sittin' on the "pick n' pour" dish
Through juniper thistles, briers
All the day you roam
The best words you heard that day
"Let's pick towards home"
Now you have picked your path
All in a row we would sway
But now it's time for supper
Of course, biscuits and tea
I guess you know the next line
"Crack a limb across your knee"

Now that winter's settled in
No limbs to be found
Sure would sound good
In the stove we gathered 'round
The puddin' is poppin' on the stove
We are waiting patiently
But one of you guys have "that look"
Don't say "Noona" to me!
You're the one that's finished
"Crack a limb across your knee"

Evenings are long
It's games we must explore
Don't forget the silly one
"Go Put Your Nose To The Door"
Trying to decide, we all begin to roam
To find that we were on "Dickie's land"
And Dickie isn't home
Than there's a good ole "Blind Man's Bluff"
Your master's horses — red, white, and blue
The only thing our master kept
Was a cow, and a chicken or two

There was one game, I do recall
We played every Saturday night
Think about it carefully
And you will say that I am right
You just finished eating
Baked beans, corn bread and butter
You know the one I have in mind —
"Blue Beans – Come And Get Your Supper"

On Sunday, sitting all cozy
Water pail filled to the brim
Reading Len Smith's Comics
Or someone strikes up a hymn
The smell of bread from the oven

Dried apples hangin' on the pole
Sippin' peppermint tea to ward off the cold
The long winter will soon be over
Spring is drawing near
You just heard what Papa said —
"Tab just washed behind his ear"

March winds have started though
The trees, branches and leaves
You are standin' on the banking
With your hands pulled up in your sleeves
Standin' on the banking
To the other side we run
No, we were not being silly!
Just following the sun!
Step on the first fast spider
Tease the slow sourbug
Feel sorry for the forgotten apple
Waiting for the first rosebud
Finally leaving the banking
Trying to do it with pride
The reason we left the banking?
Because the banking began to slide

Now, for the cranberry pickin'
Through the swamp that once was a pond
Through the cold and wet and dampness
End up on the back of "Fred John"
What with all the cranberries
You would sure bring everyone some
The reason you did not eat them?
Your hands were too "gull-darn" numb!
I think you should go back once more
Before the woods are gone
Just to gaze around and find
A stump you can sit upon
Oh yes, we are getting older now

Watch out, you may take a nap
Maybe it would be a good idea to
Lay a limb across your lap

They tried so hard to give us
All our wants and needs
They taught us "truth" and "honesty"
They taught us to "do good deeds"
They gave us their very best
But the best they gave was free
So the last words of this poem
Pertains to the others, and you and me
We wish we knew them longer
Maybe just to say "Thanks!"
So I dedicate this silly poem
Respectfully "Etta and Frankie"
—Love, Mae

TORONTO
By Christie Cromwell-Simmonds

Waiting for a streetcar at Spadina and Bloor
Toronto is so exciting!
Rush to catch the subway, just to shop at Eaton's Store
Toronto is so exciting!

The shouting of the Blue Jay fans coming home from the
   Dome
All in their white and blue
Grab a delicious hotdog on your way home
It's the Toronto thing to do.

Walk along the Boardwalk
On a hot summer's night
Toronto is so exciting!
A bum is bound to ask you for some change for a bite
Toronto is so exciting!

New City Hall; the CN Tower; Ontario Place
And don't forget The Metro Zoo
And on most city-corners, there's a beautiful old Church
Just waiting to welcome you
A kaleidoscope of colours; a beautiful sight to see
Of all nationalities
One can travel o'er the globe right on Yonge Street
Enjoying each nation's cuisine.

There's Greek food on the Danforth; New India on
Gerrard
Italian — Jamaican — and Chinese too
So satisfy your appetite at each tasty spot
It's the Toronto thing to do

Let's shout for the Raptors; or stroll the Lesly Spit
And visit Castleloma too
And don't forget the Great Exhibition
It's the Toronto thing to do

We all want to get away and go back home
It all sounds so inviting
But let's admit — we love it here in this Melting Pot
Toronto is so exciting!

"We have loved her during life, let us not abandon her, until we have conducted her by our prayers into the house of the Lord."

St. Ambrose

My Jesus, have mercy on the soul of

Christie Lorraine Cromwell-Simmonds

December 25, 1929 - April 29, 2005

PRAYER

Incline Thine ear, O Lord, unto our prayers, wherein we humbly pray Thee to show Thy mercy upon the soul of Thy servant, whom Thou hast commanded to pass out of this world, that Thou wouldst place her in the region of peace and light, and bid her to be a partaker with Thy Saints. Through Christ our Lord.

Amen.

ROSAR - MORRISON FUNERAL HOME

Appendix

The Black Loyalists

Black Loyalist history begins with the American Revolutionary War: It was 1775 and Lord Dunmore, the Royal Governor of Virginia, had a strategy to subdue the rebellious colonists. He offered freedom to any slave who would escape from his rebel master and fight on the side of those loyal to the British Crown. More than 300 Blacks immediately found their way behind British lines and formed the Ethiopian Regiment. Black Soldiers fought in the belief that they were securing freedom, not only for themselves, but for all enslaved blacks. The British were confident, because slaves made up 20% of the American population, that if they could convince them to join the ranks, the colonial uprising would be squelched.

By 1779, the British saw another reason for luring slaves from the plantations. Their departure from rebel-owned estates would seriously undermine the southern plantations' economy. The British extended their offer of freedom to include grants of land and provisions to the former slaves once the rebellion was defeated. It is estimated that as many as 100,000 slaves had taken refuge behind British lines. By the summer of 1782, it became evident that the Americans were winning the war and the British began to prepare to depart.

They left a number of Blacks behind as they retreated who were recaptured into slavery. Other Black Loyalists were resettled in Florida, the West Indies and British North America (Canada). More than 3,500, the largest group of

Black Loyalists, were transported to Nova Scotia and New Brunswick. The Loyalist colonies were not equipped to maintain the influx of thousands of new citizens. A priority system was established to serve the newest citizens to British North America. White officers and gentlemen were served first in terms of rations and land grants. Ordinary privates and labouring people, among the Whites, had to wait. The Blacks, coming up last, rarely received the land or rations promised to them.

With a population of more than 2,500, Birchtown, Nova Scotia, became the largest settlement of free blacks outside Africa. There were 649 male heads of families in Birchtown during the muster of 1784. Out of bureaucratic incompetence and racial inequality, only 184 heads of families received the promised Crown land. Their granted lands measured an average of 34 acres. Other Black Loyalists settled communities at Port Mouton (near Liverpool); Brindley Town (near Digby); Tusket and Greenville (near Yarmouth); Little Tracadie (Guysborough County); Preston (Halifax County), Annapolis Royal, Halifax and Saint John, New Brunswick.

In the eight years that followed the Black Loyalist settlement in Lower Canada, the communities suffered. Harsh climatic conditions, soil unsuitable for cultivation, high unemployment and unfair treatment from authorities were some of the hardships endured. Either Black Loyalists were located in exclusively Black settlements with farms too small to ensure self-support, or they were scattered as landless members of the White Loyalist settlements. Many Blacks were able to work as day workers for Whites. Their employers easily exploited the desperate Blacks. Wage rates for Blacks averaged one-quarter of what was acceptable for Whites. Shelburne saw the violent outcome of this system when it became the location of the first race riot in North America as disbanded White soldiers drove Blacks out of their homes in order to secure employment for themselves.

When the Sierra Leone Company entered the scene in 1791, it is unsurprising that Nova Scotia and New Brunswick saw the exodus of almost half of the Black Loyalist community. The British-formed company offered Blacks more land and a chance to establish their own governing policies in the West African country. Dissatisfied with the Canadian government's failure to provide land, support and equality among the races, 1,200 Blacks boarded ships for Sierra Leone. The Black Loyalists who stayed in British North America numbered approximately 2,500. Economically, the Black community's position showed improvement within the decade. Many Blacks completed their indenture terms, and more Blacks working as apprentices began to qualify for trades. By 1812, employers could not find enough Blacks to fill available work and wages rose accordingly. During the war of 1812, Blacks volunteered in the militia and formed three separate Black corps. The Black Loyalists, although still a disadvantaged class, were watching as slavery and racial distinctions were beginning to erode and economic advance was in sight.

The Black Loyalist Heritage Society was formally incorporated in 1991 when a few concerned citizens gathered in the interest of preserving Birchtown's historical significance, which was being threatened by a proposed landfill. They formed the Shelburne County Cultural Awareness Society, which changed its name in 1999 to the current Black Loyalist Heritage Society. The Society is a national nonprofit organization governed by a board of directors, elected annually from among the membership. Their offices are located at 104 Old Birchtown Road, in the centre of a site designated to honour Black Loyalist history. Also located on-site is the Black Burial Ground, St. Paul's Anglican Church, a Heritage Walking Trail and the Old Schoolhouse Museum and Gift Shop.

—Debra Davis-Hill, Registrar/Historian
for the Black Loyalists Heritage Society